Observation and Assessment

Join us on the web at

EarlyChildEd.delmar.com

Observation and Assessment

Barbara Ann Nilsen, Ed.D

DELMAR
CENGAGE Learning™

Australia • Brazil • Japan • Korea • Mexico • Singapore • Spain • United Kingdom • United States

DELMAR
CENGAGE Learning™

Observation and Assessment, Professional Enhancement Series
Barbara Ann Nilsen

NOTICE TO THE READER
The author and Delmar affirm that the Web site URLs referenced herein were accurate at the time of printing. However, due to the fluid nature of the Internet, we cannot guarantee their accuracy for the life of the edition.

For product information and technology assistance, contact us at **Cengage Learning Customer & Sales Support, 1-800-354-9706.**

For permission to use material from this text or product, submit all requests online at **www.cengage.com/permissions.** Further permissions questions can be emailed to **permissionrequest@cengage.com.**

Library of Congress Control Number: 2007017381

ISBN-13: 978-1-4180-7279-7

ISBN-10: 1-4180-7279-6

Delmar
10 Davis Drive
Belmont, CA 94002-3098
USA

Cengage Learning is a leading provider of customized learning solutions with office locations around the globe, including Singapore, the United Kingdom, Australia, Mexico, Brazil, and Japan. Locate your local office at **www.cengage.com/global.**

Cengage Learning products are represented in Canada by Nelson Education, Ltd.

To learn more about Delmar, visit **www.cengage.com/delmar.**

Purchase any of our products at your local college store or at our preferred online store **www.ichapters.com.**

Printed in the United States of America
3 4 5 6 7 8 9 12 11 10

TABLE OF CONTENTS

This tool was developed to help you, the budding teacher and/or child care provider, as you move into your first classroom. The editors at Thomson Delmar Learning encourage and appreciate your feedback on this or any of our other products. Go to www.earlychilded.delmar.com and click on the "Professional Enhancement series feedback" link to let us know what you think.

INTRODUCTION

You are reading this because you "just love children." You have likely been hired as a babysitter to watch children while their parents went out for an evening or even for regular periods while they were at work. You kept the children safe by watching what they did, where they went. By interacting with the children, listening to them talk, or watching how they played, you probably made some mental observations about what they could do physically and what they knew. You may have wondered about some other things, like what made the children the way they were.

Now that you are pursuing teaching as a career, that "kid watching" moves to a new level. You will be seeing each child and each group of children within the context of a program, framed by your growing knowledge of child development, and reflected against your responsibility for not only their safety but their developmental progress. You will use what you see in new ways, and will need a way to share what you see with others through some form of hard evidence, more than your own memories of what occurred. That is professional observation and assessment of children's development.

This book provides you with:

- Child development stages and developmental alerts

- Explanation of the difference between watching and observing

- Reasons for why each child is different from another

- Awareness of yourself and its impact on observation

- Common methods used to record/document what you observe

- Uses for what you have observed and recorded that assist in advancing each child's development

- Uses of classroom documentation and assessment for reporting and accountability

- Tips on managing all the paperwork you collect on each child

- Reminders about the ethics of gathering information on children

REFLECTIONS FOR DEVELOPING TEACHERS

You have probably heard the word "Reflection" before, but you may not be sure that you fully understand it when you keep seeing it in courses, textbooks, and articles in professional journals. Think of its usual meaning: You see your reflection in the mirror, the store window, the lake water, or any shiny surface. You know that is what you look like, and you recognize the image of yourself. (From the research into children's developmental milestones, we actually know that reflection is a cognitive milestone; at about the age of 12 months, a child looks into the mirror and knows it is her or himself. There is an interesting experiment using a "dot on the nose" that tells researchers this. Once a child no longer reaches for the dot he or she sees in the mirror image, but reaches for his or her own nose, it is a sign that the child knows the dot is on her own nose.) Now, back to reflection. You know it is you when you see it. So then, what's this got to do with teaching?

Reflection, or self-reflection in this context, means looking at yourself, not physically, but mentally and emotionally. What do you *think* about this? How do you *feel* about this? There is yet another step in the reflective process. It's the "so what" factor. Since this is the way you think or feel about this, what will you *do* about this? Think of it as looking in the mirror and seeing your hair askew or a piece of spinach on your tooth. Once you know about it, you are compelled to decide to act. The application to your profession of teaching is now clearer. Once you learn something, or come to think of an idea or concept in a new way, you think about its meaning, think about how you feel about it, and decide if it will lead you to act in a different way.

Take the knowledge you now have about the dot on the nose. Now that you know about this, the next time you are with a child who is about 12 months old, you might remember this little experiment. Have the child look into a mirror. Then put a dot on the child's nose and show the child the mirror again. What happened? And what does that tell you about that child? You never would have thought to try this before you learned this bit of child development knowledge. This knowledge might have heightened your curiosity about how a child would react to the mirror and the dot, so you acted on that new knowledge and on your own curiosity. When you saw what the child did, you thought again about the whole episode and drew conclusions about the child and what you might do in the future. That is self-reflection. Thinking, feeling, acting, and then thinking, feeling, and acting about that thinking and feeling. Now you get the picture. Reflective teaching is a circular thinking pattern. It is doing more than just accepting everything you see and feel, but thinking about the meaning of what you have observed and acting upon it.

Here is a bit of reflection on the introduction to the subject of observation of children:

QUESTIONS FOR REFLECTION

Reflections for Developing Teachers

People have seen me with children and tell me, "You're good with children." What did they see that led them to say that?

_____

_____

Here is a list of my characteristics that will help me be a "good" teacher.

_____

_____

Write down how you think you acquired each of the characteristics you listed.

_____

_____

Now go back to the list and think about how you can use that characteristic in your teaching.

_____

_____

Now think about some characteristics that good teachers need that are not on your list. How will you acquire them?

_____

_____

That is self-reflection. Seeing yourself as others see you, thinking more deeply about it, and then thinking about meaning and actions that might be necessary in the future.

_____

_____

By observing children (professionals call them children), I think I can tell the following about them:

_____

_____

TIPS FOR SUCCESS

Remember that you are a role model for children. They are constantly watching how you dress, what you say, and what you do.

BE A PROFESSIONAL

- Dress conservatively and follow your employer's clothing expectations (which could include wearing closed-toe shoes to be safe and active with children and clean, modest, and comfortable clothing)

- Be prepared and on time

- Avoid excessive absences

- Use appropriate language with children and adults

- Be positive when talking to parents. Show that you are forming a positive relationship with their child "catch children doing something right" and share those accomplishments. You can discuss the challenges you face with children after you have established trust with their parents.

BE A TEAM PLAYER

- Rely on team members to help you learn the parameters of your new position

- Don't be afraid to ask questions or for guidance from teammates

- Show your support and be responsible

- Step in to do your share of the work; don't expect others to clean up after you

- Help others whenever possible

- Respect others' ideas and avoid telling them how to do things

- Strive to balance your ability to make decisions with following the lead of others

LEARN ABOUT CHILDREN

- Be aware of their physical, social, emotional, and cognitive development

- Assess children's development and plan curriculum that will enhance it

- Be aware that children will test you! (Children, especially school age, will expect that you don't know the rules, and may try to convince you to let them do things that were not previously allowed.)

- Never hesitate to double-check something with teammates when in doubt

- Use positive guidance techniques with children

GUIDANCE TECHNIQUES FOR GAINING CHILDREN'S COOPERATION

There are a myriad of techniques that will help children cooperate. Children need respectful reminders of expectations and adult support in reaching those expectations. Be sure that your expectations are age appropriate and individually appropriate. These techniques are more preventive in nature:

- Use positive phrases and state exactly what you expect children to do. "Stand by the door" is more effective that "Don't go outside until everyone is ready."

- Avoid "no" and "don't." Be clear about what it is you want children to do, not what you don't want them to do.

- Sequence directions using "When-then." For example, "When things are put away where they belong, then we can go outside."

- Stay close. Merely standing near children can be enough to help them manage behavior. Be aware, however, that if you are talking to another adult, children may act out because they know they do not have your attention.

- Offer sufficient and appropriate choices. Children need a variety of activities that interest them and that will create opportunities for success.

- Create a schedule that balances children's activity with quieter periods to help them retain control.

GETTING STARTED

There is always an array of new information to learn when starting in a new position working with children, either as a student doing field work or as a new employee. Use this fill-in-the blank section to customize this resource book to your specific environment.

Important information I need to know:

What are the school's or center's hours of operation?

On school days: _____

_____

_____

On vacation days: _____

_____

_____

What is the basic daily schedule, and what are my responsibilities during each time segment?

_____

_____

_____

_____

_____

_____

What are the procedures for checking children in and out of the program?

_____

_____

_____

Do I call if I have to be absent? Who is my contact?

Name: _____

Phone number: _____

What is the dress code for employees?

_____

_____

_____

For what basic health and safety practices will I be responsible? Where are the materials stored for this? (Bleach, gloves, etc.)

Sanitizing tables: _____

_____

_____

_____

Cleaning and maintaining of equipment and materials: _____

_____

_____

_____

What are the emergency procedures?

Mildly injured child: _____

_____

_____

_____

_____

Earthquake/tornado: _____

_____

_____

_____

_____

Fire: _____

_____

_____

_____

_____

_____

First aid: _____

_____

_____

_____

_____

Unauthorized, suspicious, or dangerous person in the building:

_____

_____

_____

_____

Other: _____

_____

_____

_____

_____

Observation and Assessment Questions to Ask

What methods of observation and documentation does the program currently use?

_____

_____

_____

What is the formal screening or assessment tools currently used?

_____

_____

_____

Does the program have signed family permission forms for observation, photography, and videography?

_____

_____

Where are children's records stored? Who has access to them? What access will I have?

_____

_____

_____

As a student, what times in the schedule are best to observe children in free play? In routines? In teacher-directed activities? In one-on-one activities? In group activities?

_____

_____

_____

OBSERVATION ETIQUETTE

When you are a student with observation/recording assignments consider the following suggestions to act in a professional and ethical manner:

- Seek permission in writing from parent/family, school administrator, and child where it is appropriate to the facility and situation.

- Inquire and comply with background checks and/or formal orientation that may be required of students or volunteers.

- Sign in and out. Provide proper identification. All visitors to schools, child care centers and family child care homes should sign in and out on a log if one is provided for that purpose. Additionally, observers should wear a badge or nametag with proper identification so that others know that they are visiting the program with permission.

- Conduct yourself in a professional manner. Arrive for observations on time, fully prepared, and appropriately dressed.

- Respect the role of other adults present during the observation. To avoid tampering with the natural setting, the observer should not spend undue time discussing the child with the teacher during the observation. Discussing the child with the family is the teacher's role, not yours, since you see only a limited view of the child. Avoid offering teaching or guidance instruction. Avoid judging the teacher, family, or program.

- Respect the child. Understand that the child may feel unsure about your presence in his or her environment. Be unobtrusive so the child does not "feel" watched, as this may change behavior and make the child uncomfortable.

- Only enter play when invited by the child, and approved by the teacher.

- Observe the child in the familiar, secure setting. Do not remove the child to another room for individual observation or assessment.

- Keep all information about children, families, and the program confidential.

- If you believe that practices may be harmful to children, take those concerns directly to your instructor and do not discuss them with anyone else.

Adapted from Ahola, D., & Kovacik, A. (2007). *Observing and understanding child development: A child study manual.* Clifton Park, NY: Delmar.

Whatever method you select, you must gather the materials you need to carry out your plan. Make sure you have these readily available:

- Pen/pencils
- Paper
    - School-lined paper for anecdotal/running records
    - Graph paper for sketching room layout or drawing block structures
    - Sticky notes to write short notes to place in a child's file
    - Index cards (if this is your selected way of recording)
    - Mailing labels to write short notes to place in a child's file
- Writing surface such as a clip board or pad within a folder—this helps keep your observations concealed and private
- Forms—whatever you have selected to use such as checklists, class list logs, time samples, rating scales
- Calendar to remember the date and to make your observation plan
- Camera
- Audio/video recorder with blank tapes

CHAPTER

1

OBSERVATION VS. WATCHING CHILDREN

Everyone watches children. Adults are programmed to find the youngest of the species interesting to watch. However, not everyone watches in the same context. A parent watches his or her child with keen interest, and with heart-swelling pride in each accomplishment. The store clerk (who has been warned that children have been stealing from the store) watches a child to be sure no little thing is slipped into the pocket. The physician watches a child for signs of illness, disease, or physical or developmental irregularities. The teacher watches in a different way. This watching fulfills many purposes, reflecting on what is seen, trying to make meaning, and then deciding what to do based on what is seen. (Professionals watch "children." Words are powerful, and using "child" and "children" rather than "kid" or "kids" is a small way that you show respect for your "clients.")

EXERCISE

In a public place, such as a grocery store or the mall, find five different people who are looking at a child. What situation brings them to watch that child? What are they looking for? Do they take any actions based on what they see?

WHAT CAN WE LEARN FROM WATCHING?

We can answer a lot of questions about a child from watching that child:

Question About the Child	Clues to the Answer
How old is this child?	
What is the child's gender?	
What language does the child speak?	
What is the child's race or ethnic group?	
How is the child's coordination?	
What are the child's interests?	
How is the child's attention span?	
What does the child already know?	
Does the child have any disabilities?	
How curious is the child?	
Is the child creative?	
How does the child get along with other children?	
Is the child with a group that looks like it could be the child's family?	
If so, how is the child interacting with family members?	

EXERCISE

In a public place, select a child and make notes on what you can learn about the child by watching. Be careful that you don't call attention to yourself or you may be approached by security.

THINKING ABOUT WHAT WE SEE

Now we move from watching to observation. From what you saw in the child you watched, think about the following:

- **APPROXIMATE AGE**—What clue gave you indications of the child's age? Could the child be smaller than most children that age? What might account for that? Given the child's smaller stature, what effect does that have on the child's other abilities? Because the child is smaller than other children that age, do people treat the child differently? What would you have to do as a teacher to effectively interact with this child?

- **ABILITIES**—What exactly did the child do that indicates the child's competence? How did the child learn or develop those abilities? What might have hindered the child from learning or developing abilities like other children? If you were the teacher with that child in your group, how would you react to the child? How would you discuss the child's abilities with the family?

- **INTERESTS**—How intense is the child's interest in objects or the environment? Is the child fully engaged, or easily distracted? What does the child focus on, people or things? If you were the teacher, how would you help the child attend to concepts or lessons that you set as your objective for the child or the group?

- **SOCIABILITY**—Is the child interacting with other children or adults? Does the child seem competent in making his or her needs and wants known? Does the child exhibit any concern for the needs of others or is the child totally self-centered? Does the child appear aggressive toward others? What does the child do to get the attention or interact with others? As the teacher of this child, what effect might this child's behavior have on others and how would you have to structure the environment and your interactions with the child to promote good social skills?

- **LANGUAGE**—Do you hear the child speaking in English or in another language? If you understand the child, is the child's speech clear and understandable? Is the child using vocabulary and grammar appropriate for the child's age? Does the child use language to express needs, wants, ideas, and feelings? If this child were in your class, how would you carry on a conversation with the child that could help build a relationship between you and the child?

Observation involves closely watching, listening, and then thinking (reflecting) on the meaning of what we have observed based on what we know about child development. It eventually helps the teacher form a deep knowledge of the child, assessing the child in every developmental domain (not just for the knowing). The teacher evaluates the developmental level of the decision-making that follows to plan a learning environment and activities to help the child practice skills already acquired, and to develop new ones. The teacher again uses observation to then evaluate how the child is progressing along the developmental or learning continuum.

It's impossible to keep all the details of the observation in one's memory, so reflections must be written down (recorded). You will read more about that later.

WHY NOT JUST GIVE THEM A TEST?

This is a question that many people ask. You probably have a lot of experience taking tests. Probably the results were varied. On some tests you did very well. Congratulations! On others you did not do so well. Why not?

● ● ● ● ● ● ● *Think About It* ● ● ● ● ● ● ● ●

- **What might be some reasons why you did not do well on a test?**

Some reasons may include:

- **Not feeling well**

- **Hungry**

- **Not enough rest**

- **The room was too hot/cold/noisy**

- **The directions were confusing**

- **You could not concentrate because you were afraid/sad/excited/nervous**

- **The person giving the test made you uncomfortable**

- **You were a stranger to the place where the test was given**

- **You felt there was a lot of pressure riding on this test**

- **You didn't care how you did**

- **You didn't know the answer**

All of those things have affected us when we have taken tests. But these factors are magnified for young children who are taking a test. The outcome is that the results may not be an accurate indication of what the person knows or can do. Young children do not have the attention span or physical small muscle ability for a sit-down, paper and pencil test. Other kinds of test results can be affected by so many factors that have nothing to do with the child's ability or knowledge, that the test is useless. That is why observation and recording is the preferred way of evaluating what a child knows and can do. This is called "authentic assessment." It is authentic because it takes place within the normal setting and routine of the child's day. While the child is performing regular activities, he or she is observed by a person who is well known to the child, has a background in child development, knows the child well, and can tell if this is normal or unusual behavior for the child. Some standardized assessments may meet these criteria. You can read more about this in Chapter 4.

GUIDELINES FOR ASSESSMENT

Consider whether observation or testing yields the best information about a child.

	Direct Observation	Standardized Test
1. Is the assessment based on the goals and objectives of the program and curriculum used?		
2. Are the results to benefit children (individualize instruction, identify interests and needs?		
3. Does the assessment address all domains of development as well as children's feelings and dispositions toward learning?		

	Direct Observation	Standardized Test
4. Does the assessment provide useful information to teachers to help them do a better job?		
5. Does the assessment procedure rely on periodic performances to reflect children's development over time?		
6. Is the assessment conducted as a part of the ongoing classroom activity?		
7. Is the assessment based on the child's overall capabilities or on skills in isolation from one another?		
8. Does the assessment rely on multiple sources of information?		
9. Does the assessment reflect individual, cultural, and linguistic diversity?		
10. Are children comfortable and relaxed during assessment?		
11. Do the families feel supported, not threatened, by the assessment process?		
12. Does the assessment focus on the child's strengths and capabilities rather than deficits?		
13. Is the teacher the primary assessor and adequately trained for this role?		
14. Does the assessment process involve collaboration among teachers, children, families, and administrators?		
15. Do families contribute information to the assessment and are they informed of the assessment's findings about their own child, not in comparison to other children?		

	Direct Observation	Standardized Test
16. Do children have an opportunity to reflect on and evaluate their own learning?		
17. Does the assessment include what the child can perform individually as well as with assistance?		
18. Is the assessment part of a systematic collection of data used for planning instruction and communicating with families?		

Adapted from the Position Statement on Early Childhood Curriculum, Assessment, and Program Evaluation, 2003. National Association for the Education of Young Children (NAEYC) and the National Association of Early Childhood Specialists in State Departments of Education (NAECS/SDE). www.naeyc.org.

Child observation, recording, and assessments are tied to children's daily activities, both what they can do on their own and with adult prompting and support. Infants and toddlers are observed during routines and activities; preschoolers and older children are observed during unstructured playtimes, routines, planned classroom experiences, and instruction. In a later section you will read more about standardized tests as an assessment tool.

EXERCISE

As a teacher, think about why observing children will be more than just an interesting thing to do. Think about the following reasons for closely observing the children for whom you are responsible. What might you observe and then what resultant action might you need to take?

WHY OBSERVE	MIGHT SEE	ACTION
Promote safety		
Promote good health		
Help with difficult task		
Behavior "against the rules"		

WHY OBSERVE	MIGHT SEE	ACTION
Discover the child's interests		
Discover how the child learns best		
Encourage the child to meet a challenge		
Discuss what the child is doing		
Measure the child's progress in learning and development		
Plan activities that the child can manage and be interested in		
Be able to tell the family that the child accomplished something that day		
Show the program administrator that you are helping children learn		
Understand how the children are reacting to your planned learning activities		
Be responsive to suspicious wounds on the child's face, arms, and legs		

QUESTIONS FOR REFLECTION

Observation vs. Watching Children

1. Complete this sentence: I like watching (observing) children best when they are _____.

   _____ years old

   male or female

   acting like…

   playing at…

   I think this is because _____.

2. Whenever I am out in a public place, I find myself watching children and their families. It seems to me that most families _____ _____. That might be because _____.

3. My view on testing is _____. This is because _____.

4. When I think about observing children in my own classroom, I know that _____.

5. I will need to use my _____ skills, my _____ knowledge and my _____ when observing in my classroom.

2

EVERY CHILD IS DIFFERENT

Even families of identical twins will confirm the fact that each child is unique. Although each child is an individual, all children share certain characteristics and abilities at approximately the same age. Understanding the universal patterns of child development is vital when it comes to observing children. You have to know what you're seeing when you see it. For example, have you ever seen the ultrasound of an unborn child? It just looks like black smears and smudges, until someone points out the head, or the arm. Then you might see it. You have to have a frame of reference, knowledge that helps you know what to look for, or to interpret what you see.

Here's another example. Read this word: fovea. You can see it, read it, and even pronounce it because you have phonetic knowledge, but unless you know its meaning, the word is just a visual and auditory image. It means "a small depression or fossil." (You know, those rocks that have holes in them. The hole is a fovea. Ah, now you know.) Observing children without the knowledge of child development is like looking at the sonogram or the word fovea. You can see, but what you see has little meaning. People may watch children all the time, but those with child development knowledge can tell what stage the child is in, what comes next, and if there is a developmental lag. This is a "specialized body of knowledge" that comes from the study of the various developmental domains. It serves as the lens through which you observe children, and it becomes an unconscious comparison between what you see and what you know.

CHILD DEVELOPMENT STAGES

When we talk about child development stages, we refer to research conducted by hundreds and thousands of people who have discovered commonalities among children of certain ages related to specific areas or domains. Over time, researchers have come to the conclusion that physically, socially, emotionally, sexually, intellectually, linguistically, and creatively all human species develop in a similar pattern over time. So while every child is different, every child is the same in some ways. This is a *big idea* because it means that once a person has some basic knowledge of child development, that person can observe a child, make some substantial judgments about the child's age, and then determine if the areas of development are in agreement with the chronological age. Some of this knowledge is pretty well known by everyone.

Here is an overview of some developmental domains and the theorists or researchers whose work is widely accepted (see Figure 2–1). You will learn about each of them in your courses in child development and early childhood education as well as in psychology, sociology, and history.

Piaget's Stages of Cognitive Development	Stages of Art Kellogg; Lowenfeld and Brittain; Schirrmacher	Language Development	Writing/ Reading	Erikson's Psycho-social Stages
Sensorimotor (b–24 months) Moving from reflexes to object permanence	Scribbling and mark-making (b–2 years) Random exploration Nonintentional	Pre/Language (b–2 years) Sounds, telegraphic sentences	Book Handling Skills (b–2 years) Right side up, front/back, turn pages	Basic Trust vs. Mistrust (b–2 years) Consistent experiences
Preoperational 2–7 years Egocentric Representation of objects and events by appearances	Personal Symbol and Design (2–4 years) Controlled scribbling, named scribbling	Beginning Language (2–4 years) Acquiring vocabulary, grammar, social speech	Function of print (2–4 years) Reads symbols in context Read pictures Beginning writing	Autonomy vs. Shame/Doubt (2–4 years) Independence, sensory exploration
	Preschematic (4–7 years) Generalized symbols recognizable to others Nonrepresentational	Language (4–7 years) Symbolic language Humor	Readers and Writers (5–8 years) Decode print Invented spelling Word identity	Initiative vs. Guilt (4–7 years) Constructive activities, own decisions
Concrete Operational (7–11 years) Logical, concrete thinkers. Can conserve	Schematic/Realism (7–9 years) Representation of what he knows, not necessarily what he sees			Industry vs. Inferiority (7 years to puberty) Sense of duty, academic

Figure 2–1   Theorist comparison chart.

EXERCISE

Give yourself this test:

You observe a child whose head lolls around on its neck and who must be supported by an adult. You know this child is:

    (a) newborn   (b) 1 year old   (c) 2 years old

You observe a girl who has begun to develop breasts. You know this child is:

    (a) 2 years old   (b) 10 years old   (c) 18 years old

You observe a child who is standing upright and walking with legs wide apart, most of the time holding onto furniture. You know this child is:

    (a) 1 year old   (b) 3 years old   (c) 8 years old

You probably passed the test because most people know that a newborn has to have its head supported, a 10-year-old girl is entering puberty and starting to develop breasts, and a 1 year old is walking or almost walking alone.

However, there are finer points of knowledge about stages of development that are well researched, but that not everyone knows. However, the competent teacher who knows child development will have realistic expectations for teaching children of that age. In the short test above, you may have been thinking about the child with a disability who at 2 years of age still cannot support his head, the imbalance of hormones that could prevent breasts from developing even in an 18 year old, or a baby who is walking on her own at 9 months. Those variations are what make each child unique and a challenge for the teacher, parents, and health care professionals.

PRINCIPLES OF CHILD DEVELOPMENT

While you can find the domains and stages of child development in textbooks, there are some important principles to remember.

Principles of Child Development	Example	Your Example
1. Each domain (physical, social, emotional, cognitive) is closely related and influences and is influenced by each other.	You show a child a ball and say, "Ball." She takes it, rolls it and says, "Ball." Physical and cognitive domains are working together. The next time she sees a round object she'll say, "Ball." Then you might say, "Apple. It's round like a ball but it is good to eat."	
2. Development in each of the domains occurs in an orderly sequence, building on what is already acquired.	A child gains physical control of his legs to stand and walk before he can skip.	
3. While development occurs in a sequence, development in each domain does not occur at the same rate for every child. A child may be advanced in one area while delayed in another.	A child may be able to throw and catch a ball but not yet have the language development to say, "I can throw and catch the ball."	
4. Experiences may promote or delay development, with optimal learning and development occurring when physical and emotional needs are met. There are important or optimal periods for certain types of development and learning.	A child who is held for feeding and receives food adequate for good nutrition will grow physically larger and develop a trust of the person providing the food.	
5. Development moves in a predictable sequence, from simple to complex and random to organized.	A child rolls over, then crawls, then walks.	
6. Development occurs in and is influenced by the child's social and cultural world.	The teacher learns that the child lives in a family unit of four generations and that the grandparents and great-grandparents only speak a language other than English.	

Principles of Child Development	Example	Your Example
7. Children actively try to make sense and organize experiences through play, rehearsing and repeating what they have seen and heard.	A child watches her mother talk on the phone, so she picks up her shoe and says, "'ello, bye."	
8. Development/learning is affected by genetic factors as well as what happens in the child's physical and social world.	The child's body is developed for her age but she has never had the opportunity to learn how to swim.	
9. Play is important for the child's development as well as the way in which development can be observed and assessed.	The child is riding a bicycle around and around the track; she starts by pushing along with her feet and is now pedaling.	
10. Further development thrives on challenges just beyond their capabilities but not so far as to create frustration.	The father runs alongside holding the child's bicycle seat as he learns how to ride. However, if the child is only 2 years old, the challenge to master bicycle riding is usually beyond the developmental level.	
11. Children learn and demonstrate what they know in different ways.	One child learns best by moving his body as he spells words out loud. Another child learns by looking at the spelling list over and over. Another child learns best by playing a game that uses the spelling words with a friend.	
12. Children learn best when their needs (physical and emotional) are met.	The children are greeted by name at the door by the smiling teacher. She reminds them to hang their coats in the cubbies labeled with their names and photographs, then to wash their hands and go to the table where they can help themselves to breakfast.	

EXERCISE: PRINCIPLES OF DEVELOPMENT

**Here is more to think about regarding the principles of child development.
Refer back to these principles if you need a refresher.**

1. Think of each domain and how its development affects the other domains:

   a. Physical   Social
   Emotional
   Cognitive

   b. Social   Physical
   Emotional
   Cognitive

   c. Emotional   Physical
   Social
   Cognitive

   d. Cognitive   Physical
   Social
   Emotional

2. Think about the "orderly sequence" of necessary developmental tasks that
   leads up to the accomplishment of the skill in the far right of the page.

   _____

   _____ Skating

   _____

   _____ Solving an algebra problem

   _____

   _____ Installing wiring in a house

   _____

   _____ Writing a term paper

   _____

   _____ Composing a symphony

3. What might be a reason for developmental unevenness in the
   following examples?

A child can knit a scarf but not swim.

A child can speak clearly but not cut with scissors on a line.

A child can add and subtract in her head but not share her toys with her friends.

A child can read almost any written material but cannot see her mother leave without crying.

A child can draw intricate designs but is still using diapers.

4. What are some experiences that will promote development in the following domains?

Physical
Social
Emotional
Cognitive

What are some experiences that may inhibit normal development in the following domains?

Physical
Social
Emotional
Cognitive

5. When children play _____, they are learning _____.

Candyland®
Going to the doctor's office
Taking care of baby
Measuring at the sand/water table
"Reading" a book by looking at the pictures

6. Think of genetic and environmental influences and events that can affect development in each domain.

	GENETIC	ENVIRONMENTAL
PHYSICAL		
SOCIAL		
EMOTIONAL		
COGNITIVE		

7. Challenges (but not frustrations) are called the "zone of proximal development." How does each of the following items in that classification enable the child to _____ just before he or she is fully able to _____?

Swimmies
Training wheels
Velcro shoe straps
Name written on dotted lines
Placemat with tracing of table setting items

8. Which activities have you seen children use that demonstrates their learning?

Verbal explanation
Draw a picture
Play-act it out
Do well on a test
Demonstrate _____

TEMPERAMENT

Another thing that makes each child unique is his or her temperament. Some call this personality, but it is more than that. Temperament has been shown to be present at birth and thought to continue throughout life. It can be observed. Aspects of temperament are listed below. (It may help to think about someone you know—even yourself—as you review them.) All of these aspects are seen and assessed by the knowledgeable observer. When a teacher who is observing a child and planning for his or her learning knows about the child's temperament, it can help the teacher be more efficient, and may result in a more competent child. Think of modifications or adjustments you may have to make for a child because you recognize the child's individual temperament:

Temperament Components	Modifications or Adjustments
Activity level—physical motion	
Rhythmicity—regularity of biological functions	
Approach or withdrawal—initial reaction to new events	
Adaptability—flexibility after initial reaction	
Intensity of reaction—energy level of responses	
Threshold of responsiveness—intensity of stimulation needed to produce a response	
Quality of mood—general behavior	
Distractibility—outside stimulation changing ongoing behavior	
Attention span and persistence—length of time activities are maintained	

SOCIAL/CULTURAL CONTEXT

Each child is born into a family that indelibly makes that child different from any other. Each family has its own beliefs, values, language, customs, practices, and economic and social position. Assessments of infants and toddlers document their ability to learn about themselves and others, communicate, think and use their muscles, all of which incorporate families' home values, languages, experiences, and rituals. In preschoolers, assessments measure physical, social, emotional, linguistic, and cognitive areas of development that include family values and languages. In school-age children, assessments broaden across disciplines, incorporating culturally based experiences (NAEYC Position Statement 2003).

The child learns "the rules of the tribe," or how things are done in that particular family (both nuclear and extended, which includes grandparents, aunts, uncles and cousins). As the child grows older, the child's social world broadens into the neighborhood, and health, educational and religious institutions. The community is a part of the larger local, state, national, and global society. At that particular time in history, the child is influenced by and will come to influence the world around her. As we observe the child, all of these factors are a part of the tapestry that makes up the child.

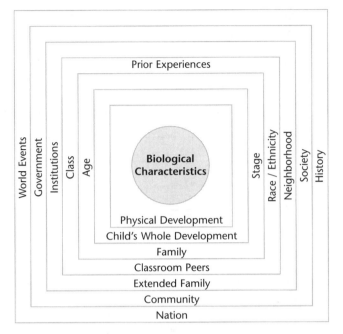

The ecological view.

1. Exercise: Think of your own social/cultural context and how
each one has influenced your life:

Biological/genetic inheritance	
Family	
Neighborhood	
Health institutions	
Educational institutions	
Religious institutions	
Local society	
State	
National society	
Global society	

Now you understand how each child in your group brings his or her
own cultural context—which may be very different from yours.

2. Exercise: Think of the various possible situations of the children in your group and how that might impact your teaching.

Family	
Neighborhood	
Health institutions	
Educational institutions	
Religious institutions	
Local society	
State	
National society	
Global society	

More and more teachers are facing a diverse population of children and families. That makes it more important than ever to recognize how cultural differences might influence the child's development, learning, and home/school relations.

EXCEPTIONALITIES

Every child is different, but some differences are more obvious than others. Some children are born with exceptionalities, and some acquire exceptionalities due to circumstances or events that occur after they are born. On one end of that spectrum are the gifted, those with exceptional intelligence or physical, social, or creative abilities. The gifted are born with the capacity to excel in a particular area and progress far beyond most other people. Sometimes this can be observed in very young children, especially by those who are familiar with the "norm."

● ● ● ● ● ● ●   *Think About It*   ● ● ● ● ● ● ●

Describe someone you know who is gifted. How can you tell that person is gifted?

What effects does being gifted have on other areas of that person's life?

At the other end of the spectrum are those who are limited in one or more developmental areas—either genetically or because of environmental factors. Identification of developmental lags or disabilities often falls on the teacher who sees the child with objective, trained eyes. Provision for these children's care and education depends on the extent of the impairment. By law, they must be placed educationally in the "least restrictive environment," where the child can perform to the maximum potential in areas where he or she is not affected, or with assistance in those areas where the child needs additional help.

⦿ ⦿ ⦿ ⦿ ⦿ ⦿ ⦿ *Think About It* ⦿ ⦿ ⦿ ⦿ ⦿ ⦿ ⦿

Describe someone you know who has a disability. How can you tell the person has a disability?

Is only one area of the person's abilities affected by the disability, or does it affect other domains of development?

Observing children can raise concerns when their developmental skills do not match expectations that are within the range of normal. Always taking into account that children's development may be uneven in areas, or may grow in spurts or lag behind, the observant teacher watches for signs that development in one area may be of special concern. Developmental measuring tools such as the checklists at the beginning of this book are extremely helpful in objectively measuring development, but they are meant only as a screening tool—an instrument that indicates that a more formal evaluation may be needed. (The child is then referred to specialists for evaluation.)

For a child with a diagnosed disability, you will be observing in order to see signs of progress in all developmental areas, taking into account the possible limitations, but helping the child to develop in all areas to his or her full potential. A child with a diagnosed disability will have an individualized education program (IEP), a written document that identifies the unique needs of the child, the special education services needed to meet those needs, short-term and annual goals, and how the child's progress will be assessed. Infants and toddlers receive an individualized family service plan (IFSP), with much family involvement.

Some types of disabilities in the various domains are:

Developmental Domain	Possible Disabilities in this Domain
Physical	Asthma—a condition affecting breathing, chronic respiratory disorder Congenital impairments—birth defects to limbs and other parts of the body affecting mobility and/or tactile functioning, includes cerebral palsy Injuries—brain, spinal cord, or other body trauma Epilepsy—brief episodes of seizures, mild to severe, losing physical control
Communication—speech, language, hearing	Deafness or severe hearing loss, blindness or severe sight loss—may be congenital or from disease or trauma Speech impairments—may be connected with other conditions such as cerebral palsy, Down syndrome, learning disabilities, stuttering, cleft palate Language delays—cognitive function, learning disabilities
Cognitive—intellectual function	Mental retardation—genetic (such as Down syndrome, fetal alcohol syndrome) or environmental (such as lead exposure or AIDS), resulting in low intellectual functioning Learning disabilities—difficulty or inability to learn, retain, use information, which may affect language, reading, math skills
Social or emotional—affects behavior, interactions with others, and school success	Emotional disturbance—inappropriate behavior, depression, unreasonable fears or phobias, sensory issues Attention deficits—learning disabilities that may affect behavior such as Attention Deficit Disorder (ADD), Attention Deficit Hyperactivity Disorder (ADHD) Autism—spectrum disorder (symptoms range from mild to severe), impairments in communication, imagination, and socialization

Think About It

Select one disability from each of the categories listed above and think about how that disability in one domain can affect other domains:

- **Physical**
- **Communication**
- **Cognitive**
- **Social Emotional**

It is the teacher's responsibility to teach *all* the children in the group. Each child will be different; the teacher needs to recognize each one's individual strengths and needs in order to maximize his or her potential.

DEVELOPMENTAL MILESTONES BY AGE

Whether you are working with infants, toddlers, preschoolers, or primary-aged children, a teacher's first requirement is to have knowledge about how children develop and learn. In your college program, you no doubt studied child development. The following is a shortened version of the universal steps most children go through as they develop. Some children will move easily from one step to another, while other children move forward in one area but lag behind in others. Use these milestones as a guide for arranging an environment and planning activities in your room.

DEVELOPMENTAL CHECKLIST

Child's Name _____   Age _____

Observer _____   Date _____

BY 6 MONTHS:	Yes	No	Sometimes
Does the child . . .			
Show continued gains in height, weight, and head circumference?			
Reach for toys or objects when they are presented?			
Begin to roll from stomach to back?			
Sit with minimal support?			
Transfer objects from one hand to the other?			
Raise up on arms, lifting head and chest, when placed on stomach?			

BY 6 MONTHS:	Yes	No	Sometimes
Babble, coo, and imitate sounds?			
Turn to locate the source of a sound?			
Focus on an object and follow its movement vertically and horizontally?			
Exhibit a blink reflex?			
Enjoy being held and cuddled?			
Recognize and respond to familiar faces?			
Begin sleeping 6 to 8 hours through the night?			
Suck vigorously when it is time to eat?			
Enjoy playing in water during bath time?			

DEVELOPMENTAL ALERTS

Check with a health care provider or early childhood specialist if, by 1 month of age, the infant *does not:*

- Show alarm or "startle" responses to loud noise.
- Suck and swallow with ease.
- Show gains in height, weight, and head circumference.
- Grasp with equal strength with both hands.
- Make eye-to-eye contact when awake and being held.
- Become quiet soon after being picked up.
- Roll head from side to side when placed on stomach.
- Express needs and emotions with cries and patterns of vocalizations that can be distinguished from one another.
- Stop crying when picked up and held.

DEVELOPMENTAL ALERTS

Check with a health care provider or early childhood specialist if, by 4 months of age, the infant *does not:*

- Continue to show steady increases in height, weight, and head circumference.
- Smile in response to the smiles of others (the social smile is a significant developmental milestone).

- Follow a moving object with eyes focusing together.
- Bring hands together over midchest.
- Turn head to locate sounds.
- Begin to raise head and upper body when placed on stomach.
- Reach for objects or familiar persons.

DEVELOPMENTAL CHECKLIST

Child's Name _____　　Age _____

Observer _____　　Date _____

BY 12 MONTHS:	Yes	No	Sometimes
Does the child . . .			
Walk with assistance?			
Roll a ball in imitation of an adult?			
Pick objects up with thumb and forefinger?			
Transfer objects from one hand to the other?			
Pick up dropped toys?			
Look directly at adult's face?			
Imitate gestures: peek-a-boo, bye-bye, pat-a-cake?			
Find object hidden under a cup?			
Feed self crackers (munching, not sucking on them)?			
Hold cup with two hands; drink with assistance?			
Smile spontaneously?			
Pay attention to own name?			
Respond to "no"?			
Respond differently to strangers and familiar persons?			

BY 12 MONTHS:	Yes	No	Sometimes
Respond differently to sounds: vacuum, phone, door?			
Look at person who speaks to him or her?			
Respond to simple directions accompanied by gestures?			
Make several consonant–vowel combination sounds?			
Vocalize back to person who has talked to him or her?			
Use intonation patterns that sound like scolding, asking, exclaiming?			
Say "da-da" or "ma-ma"?			

DEVELOPMENTAL ALERTS

Check with a health care provider or early childhood specialist if, by 12 months of age, the infant *does not:*

- Blink when fast-moving objects approach the eyes.
- Begin to cut teeth.
- Imitate simple sounds.
- Follow simple verbal requests: *come, bye-bye.*
- Pull self to a standing position.

DEVELOPMENTAL CHECKLIST

Child's Name _____   Age _____

Observer _____   Date _____

BY 2 YEARS:	Yes	No	Sometimes
Does the child . . .			
Walk alone?			
Bend over and pick up toy without falling over?			

BY 2 YEARS:	Yes	No	Sometimes
Seat self in child-size chair? Walk up and down stairs with assistance?			
Place several rings on a stick?			
Place five pegs in a pegboard?			
Turn pages two or three at a time?			
Scribble?			
Follow one-step direction involving something familiar: "Give me _____." "Show me_____." "Get a _____."?			
Match familiar objects?			
Use spoon with some spilling?			
Drink from cup holding it with one hand, unassisted?			
Chew food?			
Take off coat, shoe, sock?			
Zip and unzip large zipper?			
Recognize self in mirror or picture?			
Refer to self by name?			
Imitate adult behaviors in play—for example, feeds "baby"?			
Help put things away?			
Respond to specific words by showing what was named: toy, pet, family member?			
Ask for desired items by name: (cookie)?			
Answer with name of object when asked "What's that"?			
Make some two-word statements: "Daddy bye-bye"?			

DEVELOPMENTAL ALERTS

Check with a health care provider or early childhood specialist if, by 24 months of age, the child *does not:*

- Attempt to talk or repeat words.
- Understand some new words.
- Respond to simple questions with "yes" or "no."
- Walk alone (or with very little help).
- Exhibit a variety of emotions: anger, delight, fear.
- Show interest in pictures.
- Recognize self in mirror.
- Attempt self-feeding: hold own cup to mouth and drink.

DEVELOPMENTAL CHECKLIST

Child's Name _____   Age _____

Observer _____   Date _____

BY 3 YEARS:	Yes	No	Sometimes
Does the child . . .			
Run well in a forward direction?			
Jump in place, two feet together?			
Walk on tiptoe?			
Throw ball (but without direction or aim)?			
Kick ball forward?			
String four large beads?			
Turn pages in book singly?			
Hold crayon: imitate circular, vertical, horizontal strokes?			
Match shapes?			
Demonstrate number concepts of 1 and 2?			

BY 3 YEARS:	Yes	No	Sometimes
(Can select 1 or 2; can tell if one or two objects.)			
Use spoon without spilling?			
Drink from a straw?			
Put on and take off coat?			
Wash and dry hands with some assistance?			
Watch other children; play near them; sometimes join in their play?			
Defend own possessions?			
Use symbols in play—for example, tin pan on head becomes helmet and crate becomes a spaceship?			
Respond to "Put _____ in the box," "Take the _____ out of the box"?			
Select correct item on request: big versus little; one versus two?			
Identify objects by their use: show own shoe when asked, "What do you wear on your feet?"			
Ask questions?			
Tell about something with functional phrases that carry meaning: "Daddy go airplane."			
"Me hungry now"?			

DEVELOPMENTAL ALERTS

Check with a health care provider or early childhood specialist if, by the third birthday, the child *does not:*

- Eat a fairly well-rounded diet, even though amounts are limited. Walk confidently with few stumbles or falls; climb steps with help.

- Avoid bumping into objects.

- Carry out simple, two-step directions: "Come to Daddy and bring your book"; express desires; ask questions.

- Point to and name familiar objects; use two- or three-word sentences.

- Enjoy being read to.

- Show interest in playing with other children: watching, perhaps imitating.

- Indicate a beginning interest in toilet training.

- Sort familiar objects according to a single characteristic, such as type, color, or size.

DEVELOPMENTAL CHECKLIST

Child's Name _____   Age _____

Observer _____   Date _____

BY 4 YEARS:	Yes	No	Sometimes
Does the child . . .			
Walk on a line?			
Balance on one foot briefly? Hop on one foot?			
Jump over an object 6 inches high and land on both feet together?			
Throw ball with direction?			
Copy circles and Xs?			
Match six colors?			
Count to 5?			
Pour well from pitcher? Spread butter, jam with knife?			
Button, unbutton large buttons?			
Know own sex, age, last name?			
Use toilet independently and reliably?			
Wash and dry hands unassisted?			
Listen to stories for at least 5 minutes?			
Draw head of person and at least one other body part?			
Play with other children?			

BY 4 YEARS:	Yes	No	Sometimes
Share, take turns (with some assistance)?			
Engage in dramatic and pretend play?			
Respond appropriately to "Put it beside," "Put it under"?			
Respond to two-step directions: "Give me the sweater and put the shoe on the floor"?			
Respond by selecting the correct object—for example, hard versus soft object?			
Answer "if," "what," and "when" questions?			
Answer questions about function: "What are books for"?			

DEVELOPMENTAL ALERTS

Check with a health care provider or early childhood specialist if, by the fourth birthday, the child *does not:*

- Have intelligible speech most of the time; have children's hearing checked if there is any reason for concern.

- Understand and follow simple commands and directions.

- State own name and age.

- Enjoy playing near or with other children.

- Use three- to four-word sentences.

- Ask questions.

- Stay with an activity for 3 or 4 minutes; play alone several minutes at a time.

- Jump in place without falling.

- Balance on one foot, at least briefly.

- Help with dressing self.

DEVELOPMENTAL CHECKLIST

Child's Name _____   Age _____

Observer _____   Date _____

BY 5 YEARS:	Yes	No	Sometimes
Does the child . . .			
Walk backward, heel to toe?			
Walk up and down stairs, alternating feet?			
Cut on line?			
Print some letters?			
Point to and name three shapes?			
Group common related objects: shoe, sock, and foot: apple, orange, and plum?			
Demonstrate number concepts to 4 or 5?			
Cut food with a knife: celery, sandwich?			
Lace shoes?			
Read from story picture book—in other words, tell story by looking at pictures?			
Draw a person with three to six body parts?			
Play and interact with other children; engage in dramatic play that is close to reality?			
Build complex structures with blocks or other building materials?			
Respond to simple three-step directions: "Give me the pencil, put the book on the table, and hold the comb in your hand"?			
Respond correctly when asked to show penny, nickel, and dime?			
Ask "How" questions?			
Respond verbally to "Hi" and "How are you"?			

BY 5 YEARS:	Yes	No	Sometimes
Tell about event using past and future tenses?			
Use conjunctions to string words and phrases together—for example, "I saw a bear and a zebra and a giraffe at the zoo"?			

DEVELOPMENTAL ALERTS

Check with a health care provider or early childhood specialist if, by the fifth birthday, the child *does not*:

- State own name in full.

- Recognize simple shapes: circle, square, triangle.

- Catch a large ball when bounced (have child's vision checked).

- Speak so as to be understood by strangers (have child's hearing checked).

- Have good control of posture and movement.

- Hop on one foot.

- Appear interested in, and responsive to, surroundings.

- Respond to statements without constantly asking to have them repeated.

- Dress self with minimal adult assistance; manage buttons, zippers.

- Take care of own toilet needs; have good bowel and bladder control with infrequent accidents.

DEVELOPMENTAL CHECKLIST

Child's Name _____   Age _____

Observer _____   Date _____

BY 6 YEARS:	Yes	No	Sometimes
Does the child . . .			
Walk across a balance beam?			
Skip with alternating feet?			
Hop for several seconds on one foot?			

BY 6 YEARS:	Yes	No	Sometimes
Cut out simple shapes?			
Copy own first name?			
Show well-established handedness; demonstrate consistent right- or left-handedness?			
Sort objects on one or more dimensions: color, shape, or function?			
Name most letters and numerals?			
Count by rote to 10; know what number comes next?			
Dress self completely; tie bows?			
Brush teeth unassisted?			
Have some concept of clock time in relation to daily schedule?			
Cross street safely?			
Draw a person with head, trunk, legs, arms, and features; often add clothing details?			
Play simple board games?			
Engage in cooperative play with other children, involving group decisions, role assignments, rule observance?			
Use construction toys, such as Legos, blocks, to make recognizable structures?			
Do 15-piece puzzles?			
Use all grammatical structures: pronouns, plurals, verb tenses, conjunctions?			
Use complex sentences; carry on conversations?			

DEVELOPMENTAL ALERTS

Check with a health care provider or early childhood specialist if, by the sixth birthday, the child *does not:*

- Alternate feet when walking up and down stairs.
- Speak in a moderate voice; neither too loud, too soft, too high, too low.

- Follow simple directions in stated order: "Please go to the cupboard, get a cup, and bring it to me."
- Use four to five words in acceptable sentence structure.
- Cut on a line with scissors.
- Sit still and listen to an entire short story (5 to 7 minutes).
- Maintain eye contact when spoken to (unless this is a cultural taboo).
- Play well with other children.
- Perform most self-grooming tasks independently: brush teeth, wash hands and face.

DEVELOPMENTAL CHECKLIST

Child's Name _____   Age _____

Observer _____   Date _____

BY 7 YEARS:	Yes	No	Sometimes
Does the child . . .			
Concentrate on completing puzzles and board games?			
Ask many questions?			
Use correct verb tenses, word order, and sentence structure in conversation?			
Correctly identify right and left hands?			
Make friends easily?			
Show some control of anger, using words instead of physical aggression?			
Participate in play that requires teamwork and rule observance?			
Seek adult approval for efforts?			
Enjoy reading and being read to?			
Use pencil to write words and numbers?			

BY 7 YEARS:	Yes	No	Sometimes
Sleep undisturbed through the night?			
Catch a tennis ball, walk across balance beam, hit ball with bat?			
Plan and carry out simple projects with minimal adult help?			
Tie own shoes?			
Draw pictures with greater detail and sense of proportion?			
Care for own personal needs with some adult supervision? Wash hands? Brush teeth? Use toilet? Dress self?			
Show some understanding of cause-and-effect concepts?			

DEVELOPMENTAL ALERTS

Check with a health care provider or early childhood specialist if, by the seventh birthday, the child *does not:*

- Show signs of ongoing growth: increasing height and weight; continuing motor development, such as running, jumping, balancing.

- Show some interest in reading and trying to reproduce letters, especially own name.

- Follow simple, multiple-step directions: "Finish your book, put it on the shelf, and then get your coat on."

- Follow through with instructions and complete simple tasks: putting dishes in the sink, picking up clothes, finishing a puzzle. *Note:* All children forget. Task incompletion is not a problem unless a child *repeatedly* leaves tasks unfinished.

- Begin to develop alternatives to excessive use of inappropriate behaviors in order to get own way.

- Develop a steady decrease in tension-type behaviors that may have developed with starting school: repeated grimacing or facial tics; eye twitching; grinding of teeth; regressive soiling or wetting; frequent stomachaches; refusing to go to school.

DEVELOPMENTAL CHECKLIST

Child's Name _____   Age _____

Observer _____   Date _____

BY 8 AND 9 YEARS:	Yes	No	Sometimes
Does the child . . .			
Have energy to play, continuing growth, few illnesses?			
Use pencil in a deliberate and controlled manner?			
Express relatively complex thoughts in a clear and logical fashion?			
Carry out multiple four- to five-step instructions?			
Become less easily frustrated with own performance?			
Interact and play cooperatively with other children?			
Show interest in creative expression—telling stories, jokes, writing, drawing, singing?			
Use eating utensils with ease?			
Have a good appetite? Show interest in trying new foods?			
Know how to tell time?			
Have control of bowel and bladder functions?			
Participate in some group activities—games, sports, plays?			
Want to go to school? Seem disappointed if must miss a day?			
Demonstrate beginning skills in reading, writing, and math?			
Accept responsibility and complete work independently?			
Handle stressful situations without becoming overly upset?			

DEVELOPMENTAL ALERTS

Check with a health care provider or early childhood specialist if, by the eighth birthday, the child *does not:*

- Attend to the task at hand; show longer periods of sitting quietly, listening, responding appropriately.

- Follow through on simple instructions.

- Go to school willingly most days (of concern are excessive complaints about stomachaches or headaches when getting ready for school).

- Make friends (observe closely to see if the child plays alone most of the time or withdraws consistently from contact with other children).

- Sleep soundly most nights (frequent and recurring nightmares or bad dreams are usually at a minimum at this age).

- Seem to see or hear adequately at times (squints, rubs eyes excessively, asks frequently to have things repeated).

- Handle stressful situations without undue emotional upset (excessive crying, sleeping or eating disturbances, withdrawal, frequent anxiety).

- Assume responsibility for personal care (dressing, bathing, feeding self) most of the time.

- Show improved motor skills.

DEVELOPMENTAL ALERTS

Check with a health care provider or early childhood specialist if, by the ninth birthday, the child *does not:*

- Exhibit a good appetite and continued weight gain (some children, especially girls, may already begin to show early signs of an eating disorder).

- Experience fewer illnesses.

- Show improved motor skills in terms of agility, speed, and balance.

- Understand abstract concepts and use complex thought processes to problem-solve.

- Enjoy school and the challenge of learning.

- Follow through on multiple-step instructions.

- Express ideas clearly and fluently.

- Form friendships with other children and enjoy participating in group activities.

DEVELOPMENTAL CHECKLIST

Child's Name _____   Age _____

Observer _____   Date _____

BY 10 AND 11 YEARS:	Yes	No	Sometimes
Does the child . . .			
Continue to increase in height and weight?			
Exhibit improving coordination: running, climbing, riding a bike, writing?			
Handle stressful situations without becoming overly upset or violent?			
Construct sentences using reasonably correct grammar: nouns, adverbs, verbs, adjectives?			
Understand concepts of time, distance, space, volume?			
Have one or two "best friends"?			
Maintain friendships over time?			
Approach challenges with a reasonable degree of self-confidence?			
Play cooperatively and follow group instructions?			
Begin to show an understanding of moral standards: right from wrong, fairness, honesty, good from bad?			
Look forward to, and enjoy, school?			
Appear to hear well and listen attentively?			
Enjoy reasonably good health, with few episodes of illness or health-related complaints?			
Have a good appetite and enjoy mealtimes?			
Take care of own personal hygiene without assistance?			
Sleep through the night, waking up refreshed and energetic?			

DEVELOPMENTAL ALERTS

Check with a health care provider or early childhood specialist if, by the eleventh birthday, the child *does not:*

- Continue to grow at a rate appropriate for the child's gender.

- Show continued improvement of fine motor skills.

- Make or keep friends.

- Enjoy going to school and show interest in learning (have children's hearing and vision tested; vision and hearing problems affect children's ability to learn and their interest in learning).

- Approach new situations with reasonable confidence.

- Handle failure and frustration in a constructive manner.

- Sleep through the night or experience prolonged problems with bedwetting, nightmares, or sleepwalking.

DEVELOPMENTAL CHECKLIST

Child's Name _____ Age _____

Observer _____ Date _____

BY 12 AND 13 YEARS:	Yes	No	Sometimes
Does the child . . .			
Appear to be growing: increasing height and maintaining a healthy weight (not too thin or too heavy)?			
Understand changes associated with puberty or have an opportunity to learn and ask questions?			
Complain of headaches or blurred vision?			
Have an abnormal posture or curving of the spine?			
Seem energetic and not chronically fatigued?			
Stay focused on a task and complete assignments?			
Remember and carry out complex instructions?			
Sequence, order, and classify objects?			

BY 12 AND 13 YEARS:	Yes	No	Sometimes
Use longer and more complex sentence structure?			
Engage in conversation; tell jokes and riddles?			
Enjoy playing organized games and team sports?			
Respond to anger-invoking situations without resorting to violence or physical aggression?			
Begin to understand and solve complex mathematical problems?			
Accept blame for actions on most occasions?			
Enjoy competition?			
Accept and carry out responsibility in a dependable manner?			
Go to bed willingly and wake up refreshed?			
Take pride in appearance; keep self reasonably clean?			

DEVELOPMENTAL ALERTS

Check with a health care provider or early childhood specialist if, by the thirteenth birthday, the child *does not*:

- Have movements that are smooth and coordinated.
- Have energy sufficient for playing, riding bikes, or engaging in other desired activities.
- Stay focused on tasks at hand.
- Understand basic cause-and-effect relationships.
- Handle criticism and frustration with a reasonable response (physical aggression and excessive crying could be an indication of other, underlying problems).
- Exhibit a healthy appetite (frequent skipping of meals is not typical for this age group).
- Make and keep friends.

(Content in this section is adapted from Allen, K. E., & Marotz, L. (2007). Developmental profiles: Pre-birth through twelve, 5th ed. Clifton Park, NY: Delmar.)

DEVELOPMENTAL MILESTONES BY SKILL

As with the list of milestones by age, this list is not exhaustive, but it can be used to arrange an environment or to plan activities in your room.

BIRTH TO 1 MONTH

Physical	Date Observed
Engages in primarily reflexive motor activity	
Maintains "fetal" position especially when sleeping	
Holds hands in a fist; does not reach for objects	
In prone position, head falls lower than the body's horizontal line with hips flexed and arms and legs hanging down	
Has good upper body muscle tone when supported under the arms	
Cognitive	
Blinks in response to fast-approaching object	
Follows a slowly moving object through a complete 180-degree arc	
Follows objects moved vertically if close to infant's face	
Continues looking about, even in the dark	
Begins to study own hand when lying in tonic neck reflex position	
Prefers to listen to mother's voice rather than a stranger's	
Language	
Cries and fusses as major forms of communication	
Reacts to loud noises by blinking, moving (or stopping), shifting eyes, making a startle response	
Shows preference for certain sounds (music and human voices) by calming down or quieting	

Language, continued	Date Observed
Turns head to locate voices and other sounds	
Makes occasional sounds other than crying	
Social/Emotional	
Experiences a short period of alertness immediately following birth	
Sleeps 17–19 hours a day; is gradually awake and responsive for longer periods	
Likes to be held close and cuddled when awake	
Shows qualities of individuality in responding or not responding to similar situations	
Begins to establish emotional attachment or bonding with parents and caregivers	
Begins to develop a sense of security/trust with parents and caregivers; responses to different individuals vary	

1 TO 4 MONTHS

Physical	Date Observed
Rooting and sucking reflexes are well developed	
In prone position, Landau reflex appears and baby raises head and upper body on arms	
Grasps with entire hand; strength insufficient to hold items	
Movements tend to be large and jerky	
Turns head side to side when in a supine (face up) position	
Begins rolling from front to back by turning head to one side and allowing trunk to follow	
Cognitive	
Fixes on a moving object held at 12 inches (30.5 cm)	
Continues to gaze in direction of moving objects that have disappeared	
Exhibits some sense of size/color/shape recognition of objects in the immediate environment	
Alternates looking at an object, at one or both hands, and then back at the object	
Moves eyes from one object to another.	
Focuses on small object and reaches for it; usually follows own hand movements	

Language	Date Observed
Reacts to sounds (voice, rattle, doorbell); later will search for source by turning head	
Coordinates vocalizing, looking, and body movements in face-to-face exchanges with parent or caregiver	
Babbles or coos when spoken to or smiled at	
Imitates own sounds and vowel sounds produced by others.	
Laughs out loud	
Social/Emotional	
Imitates, maintains, terminates, and avoids interactions	
Reacts differently to variations in adult voices	
Enjoys being held and cuddled at times other than feeding and bedtime	
Coos, gurgles, and squeals when awake	
Smiles in response to a friendly face or voice	
Entertains self for brief periods by playing with fingers, hands, and toes	

4 TO 8 MONTHS

Physical	Date Observed
Parachute reflex appears toward the end of this stage; swallowing reflex appears	
Uses finger and thumb (pincer grip) to pick up objects	
Reaches for objects with both arms simultaneously; later reaches with one hand	
Transfers objects from one hand to the other; grasps object using palmar grasp	
Handles, shakes, and pounds objects; puts everything in mouth	
Sits alone without support (holds head erect, back straight, arms propped forward for support)	
Cognitive	
Turns toward and locates familiar voices and sounds	
Uses hand, mouth, and eyes in coordination to explore own body, toys, and surroundings	
Imitates actions, such as pat-a-cake, waving bye-bye, and playing peek-a-boo	
Shows fear of falling from high places, such as changing table, stairs	

Cognitive, continued	Date Observed
Looks over side of crib or high chair for objects dropped; delights in repeatedly throwing objects overboard for adult to retrieve	
Bangs objects together playfully; bangs spoon or toy on table	
Language	
Responds appropriately to own name and simple requests, such as "eat," "wave bye-bye"	
Imitates some nonspeech sounds, such as cough, tongue click, lip smacking	
Produces a full range of vowels and some consonants: r, s, z, th, and w	
Responds to variations in the tone of voice of others	
Expresses emotions (pleasure, satisfaction, anger) by making different sounds	
Babbles by repeating same syllable in a series: ba, ba, ba.	
Social/Emotional	
Delights in observing surroundings; continuously watches people and activities	
Begins to develop an awareness of self as a separate individual from others	
Becomes more outgoing and social in nature: smiles, coos, reaches out	
Distinguishes among, and responds differently to, strangers, teachers, parents, siblings	
Responds differently and appropriately to facial expressions: frowns; smiles	
Imitates facial expressions, actions, and sounds	

8 TO 12 MONTHS

Physical	Date Observed
Reaches with one hand leading to grasp an offered object or toy	
Manipulates objects, transferring them from one hand to the other	
Explores new objects by poking with one finger	
Uses deliberate pincer grip to pick up small objects, toys, and finger foods	
Stacks objects; also places objects inside one another	
Releases objects by dropping or throwing; cannot intentionally put an object down	
Begins pulling self to a standing position; begins to stand alone	

Cognitive	Date Observed
Watches people, objects, and activities in the immediate environment	
Shows awareness of distant objects (15 to 20 feet away) by pointing at them	
Reaches for toys that are visible but out of reach	
Continues to drop first item when other toys or items are offered	
Recognizes the reversal of an object: cup upside down is still a cup	
Imitates activities: hitting two blocks together, playing pat-a-cake	
Language	
Babbles or jabbers to initiate social interaction; may shout to attract attention	
Shakes head for "no" and may nod for "yes"	
Responds by looking for voice when name is called	
Babbles in sentence-like sequences; followed by jargon (syllables/sounds with language-like inflection)	
Waves "bye-bye"; claps hands when asked	
Says "da-da" and "ma-ma"	
Social/Emotional	
Exhibits a definite fear of strangers; clings to, or hides behind, parent or caregiver ("stranger anxiety"); resists separating from familiar adult ("separation anxiety")	
Enjoys being near, and included in, daily activities of family members and teachers; is becoming more sociable and outgoing	
Enjoys novel experiences and opportunities to examine new objects	
Shows need to be picked up and held by extending arms upward, crying, or clinging to adult's legs	
Begins to exhibit assertiveness by resisting caregiver's requests; may kick, scream, or throw self on the floor	

1 YEAR OLDS

Physical	Date Observed
Crawls skillfully and quickly; gets to feet unaided	
Stands alone with feet spread apart, legs stiffened, and arms extended for support	
Walks unassisted near the end of this period (most children); falls often; not always able to maneuver around furniture or toys	

Physical, continued	Date Observed
Uses furniture to lower self to floor; collapses backward into a sitting position or falls forward on hands and then sits	
Releases an object voluntarily	
Enjoys pushing or pulling toys while walking	
Cognitive	
Enjoys object-hiding activities: early on, will search same location for a hidden object; later will search in several locations	
Passes toy to other hand when offered a second object ("crossing the midline")	
Manages three to four objects by setting an object aside (on lap or floor) when presented with a new toy	
Puts toys in mouth less often	
Enjoys looking at picture books	
Demonstrates understanding of functional relationships (objects that belong together)	
Language	
Produces considerable "jargon": combines words/sounds into speech-like patterns	
Uses one word to convey an entire thought (holophrastic speech); later, produces two-word phrases to express a complete thought (telegraphic speech)	
Follows simple directions: "Give Daddy the cup"	
Points to familiar persons, animals, and toys when asked	
Identifies three body parts if someone names them: "Show me your nose (toe, ear)"	
Indicates a few desired objects/activities by name: "bye-bye," "cookie"; verbal request is often accompanied by an insistent gesture	
Social/Emotional	
Remains friendly toward others; usually less wary of strangers	
Helps pick up and put away toys	
Plays alone for short periods and does not play cooperatively	
Enjoys being held and read to	
Imitates adult actions in play	
Enjoys adult attention; likes to know that an adult is near; gives hugs and kisses	

2 YEAR OLDS

Physical	Date Observed
Walks with a more erect, heel-to-toe pattern; can maneuver around obstacles in pathway	
Runs with greater confidence; has fewer falls	
Squats for long periods while playing	
Climbs stairs unassisted (but not with alternating feet)	
Balances on one foot (for a few moments), jumps up and down, but may fall	
Begins to achieve toilet training (depending on physical and neurological development) although accidents should still be expected; will indicate readiness for toilet training	
Cognitive	
Exhibits better coordinated eye–hand movements; can put objects together, take them apart; fit large pegs into pegboard	
Begins to use objects for purposes other than intended (pushes block around as boat)	
Completes classification based on one dimension (separates toy dinosaurs from toy cars)	
Stares for long moments; seems fascinated by, or engrossed in, figuring out a situation	
Attends to self-selected activities for longer periods of time	
Shows discovery of cause and effect: squeezing the cat makes her scratch	
Language	
Enjoys being read to if allowed to point, make relevant noises, turn pages	
Realizes that language is effective for getting others to respond to needs and preferences	
Uses 50 to 300 different words; vocabulary continuously increasing	
Has broken linguistic code; in other words, much of a 2-year-old's talk has meaning to him or her	
Understands more language than can communicate verbally; most 2-year-olds' receptive language is more developed than their expressive language	
Utters three- and four-word statements; uses conventional word order to form more complete sentences	

Social/Emotional	Date Observed
Shows empathy and caring	
Continues to use physical aggression if frustrated or angry (more exaggerated in some children); physical aggression lessens as verbal skills improve	
Expresses frustration through temper tantrums; tantrum frequency peaks during this year; cannot be reasoned with while tantrum is in progress	
Finds it difficult to wait or take turns; often impatient	
Enjoys "helping" with household chores; imitates everyday activities	
Orders parents and teachers around; makes demands and expects immediate compliance	

3 YEAR OLDS

Physical	Date Observed
Walks up and down stairs unassisted using alternating feet; may jump from bottom step, landing on both feet	
Balances momentarily on one foot	
Kicks a large ball, catches a large bounced ball with both arms extended	
Feeds self; needs minimal assistance	
Jumps in place	
Pedals a small tricycle or Bigwheel	
Cognitive	
Listens attentively and makes relevant comments during age-appropriate stories, especially those related to home and family events	
Likes to look at books and may pretend to "read" to others or explain pictures	
Enjoys stories with riddles, guessing, and suspense	
Points with fair accuracy to correct pictures when given sound-alike words: keys–cheese; fish–dish; mouse–mouth	
Plays realistically: feeds doll; hooks truck and trailer together	
Places eight to ten pegs in pegboard, or six round and six square blocks in form board	

Language	Date Observed
Talks about objects, events, and people not present: "Jerry has a pool in his yard"	
Talks about the actions of others: "Daddy's mowing the grass"	
Adds information to what has just been said: "Yeah, and then he grabbed it back"	
Answers simple questions appropriately	
Asks increasing numbers of questions, including location/identity of objects and people	
Uses increased speech forms to keep conversation going: "What did he do next?" "How come she hid?"	
Social/Emotional	
Seems to understand taking turns, but not always willing to do so	
Laughs frequently; is friendly and eager to please	
Has occasional nightmares and fears the dark, monsters, or fire	
Joins in simple games and group activities, sometimes hesitantly	
Talks to self often	
Uses objects symbolically in play: block of wood may be a truck, a ramp, a bat	

4 YEAR OLDS

Physical	Date Observed
Walks a straight line (tape or chalk line on the floor)	
Hops on one foot	
Pedals and steers a wheeled toy with confidence; avoids obstacles and oncoming "traffic"	
Climbs ladders, trees, playground equipment	
Jumps over objects 5 or 6 inches (12.5 to 15 cm) high; lands with both feet together	
Runs, starts, stops, and moves around obstacles with ease	
Cognitive	
Stacks at least five graduated cubes largest to smallest; builds a pyramid of six blocks	
Indicates if paired words sound the same or different: sheet–feet, ball–wall	
Names 18-20 uppercase letters near the end of this year; may be able to print several and write own name; may recognize some printed words (especially those that have special meaning)	

Cognitive, continued	Date Observed
Some begin to read simple books (alphabet books with few words per page and many pictures)	
Likes stories about how things grow and operate	
Delights in wordplay, creating silly language	
Language	
Uses the prepositions "on," "in," and "under"	
Uses possessives consistently: "hers," "theirs," "baby's"	
Answers "Whose?" "Who?" "Why?" and "How many?"	
Produces elaborate sentence structures	
Uses almost entirely intelligible speech	
Begins to correctly use the past tense of verbs: "Mommy closed the door," "Daddy went to work."	
Social/Emotional	
Is outgoing and friendly; overly enthusiastic at times	
Changes moods rapidly and unpredictably; often throws tantrum over minor frustrations; sulk over being left out	
Holds conversations and shares strong emotions with imaginary playmates or companions; invisible friends are common	
Boasts, exaggerates, and "bends" the truth with made-up stories or claims; tests limits with "bathroom" talk	
Cooperates with others; participates in group activities	
Shows pride in accomplishments; seeks frequent adult approval	

5 YEAR OLDS

Physical	Date Observed
Walks backward, heel to toe	
Walks unassisted up and down stairs, alternating feet	
Learns to turn somersaults (should be taught the right way in order to avoid injury)	
Touches toes without flexing knees	
Catches a ball thrown from 3 feet away	
Rides a tricycle or wheeled toy with speed and skillful steering; some learn to ride bicycles, usually with training wheels	

Cognitive	Date Observed
Forms rectangle from two triangular cuts	
Builds steps with set of small blocks	
Understands concept of same shape, same size	
Sorts objects on the basis of two dimensions, such as color and form	
Sorts objects so that all things in the group have a single common feature	
Understands smallest and shortest; places objects in order from shortest to tallest, smallest to largest	
Language	
Has vocabulary of 1,500 words or more	
Tells a familiar story while looking at pictures in a book	
Uses functional definitions: a ball is to bounce; a bed is to sleep in	
Identifies and names four to eight colors	
Recognizes the humor in simple jokes; makes up jokes and riddles	
Produces sentences with five to seven words; much longer sentences are not unusual	
Social/Emotional	
Enjoys friendships; often has one or two special playmates	
Shares toys, takes turns, plays cooperatively (with occasional lapses); is often quite generous	
Participates in play and activities with other children; suggests imaginative and elaborate play ideas	
Is affectionate and caring, especially toward younger or injured children and animals	
Follows directions and carries out assignments usually; generally does what parent or teacher requests	
Continues to need adult comfort and reassurance, but may be less open in seeking and accepting comfort	

6 YEAR OLDS

Physical	Date Observed
Has increased muscle strength; typically boys are stronger than girls of similar size	
Gains greater control over large and fine motor skills; movements are more precise and deliberate although some clumsiness persists	

Physical, continued	Date Observed
Enjoys vigorous physical activity: running, jumping, climbing, and throwing	
Moves constantly, even when trying to sit still	
Has increased dexterity, eye–hand coordination, and improved motor functioning, which facilitate learning to ride a bicycle, swim, swing a bat, or kick a ball	
Enjoys art projects: likes to paint, model with clay, "make things," draw and color, work with wood	
Cognitive	
Shows increased attention; works at tasks for longer periods, although concentrated effort is not always consistent	
Understands simple time markers (today, tomorrow, yesterday) or uncomplicated concepts of motion (cars go faster than bicycles)	
Recognizes seasons and major holidays and the activities associated with each	
Enjoys puzzles, counting and sorting activities, paper-and-pencil mazes, and games that involve matching letters and words with pictures	
Recognizes some words by sight; attempts to sound out words (some may read well by this time)	
Identifies familiar coins: pennies, nickels, dimes, quarters	
Language	
Loves to talk, often nonstop; may be described as a chatterbox	
Carries on adult-like conversations; asks many questions	
Learns five to ten new words daily; vocabulary consists of 10,000 to 14,000 words	
Uses appropriate verb tenses, word order, and sentence structure	
Uses language (not tantrums or physical aggression) to express displeasure: "That's mine! Give it back, you dummy."	
Talks self through steps required in simple problem-solving situations (although the "logic" may be unclear to adults)	
Social/Emotional	
Experiences mood swings: "best friends" then "worst enemies"; loving then uncooperative and irritable; especially unpredictable toward mother or primary caregiver	
Becomes less dependent on parents as friendship circle expands; still needs closeness and nurturing but has urges to break away and "grow up"	

Social/Emotional, continued	Date Observed
Needs and seeks adult approval, reassurance, and praise; may complain excessively about minor hurts to gain more attention	
Continues to be egocentric; still sees events almost entirely from own perspective: views everything and everyone as there for child's own benefit	
Easily disappointed and frustrated by self-perceived failure	
Has difficulty composing and soothing self; cannot tolerate being corrected or losing at games; may sulk, cry, refuse to play, or reinvent rules to suit own purposes	

7 YEAR OLDS

Physical	Date Observed
Exhibits large and fine motor control that is more finely tuned	
Tends to be cautious in undertaking more challenging physical activities, such as climbing up or jumping down from high places	
Practices a new motor skill repeatedly until mastered then moves on to something else	
Finds floor more comfortable than furniture when reading or watching television; legs often in constant motion	
Uses knife and fork appropriately, but inconsistently	
Tightly grasps pencil near the tip; rests head on forearm, lowers head almost to the table top when doing pencil-and-paper tasks	
Cognitive	
Understands concepts of space and time in both logical and practical ways: a year is "a long time"; 100 miles is "far away"	
Begins to grasp Piaget's concepts of conservation (the shape of a container does not necessarily reflect what it can hold)	
Gains a better understanding of cause and effect: "If I'm late for school again, I'll be in big trouble."	
Tells time by the clock and understands calendar time—days, months, years, seasons	
Plans ahead: "I'm saving this cookie for tonight."	
Shows marked fascination with magic tricks; enjoys putting on "shows" for parents and friends	

Language	Date Observed
Enjoys storytelling; likes to write short stories, tell imaginative tales	
Uses adult-like sentence structure and language in conversation; patterns reflect cultural and geographical differences	
Becomes more precise and elaborate in use of language; greater use of descriptive adjectives and adverbs	
Uses gestures to illustrate conversations	
Criticizes own performance: "I didn't draw that right," "Her picture is better than mine."	
Verbal exaggeration commonplace: "I ate ten hot dogs at the picnic."	
Social/Emotional	
Is cooperative and affectionate toward adults and less frequently annoyed with them; sees humor in everyday happenings	
Likes to be the "teacher's helper"; eager for teacher's attention and approval but less obvious about seeking it	
Seeks out friendships; friends are important, but can stay busy if no one is available	
Quarrels less often, although squabbles and tattling continue in both one-on-one and group play	
Complains that family decisions are unjust, that a particular sibling gets to do more or is given more	
Blames others for own mistakes; makes up alibis for personal shortcomings: "I could have made a better one, but my teacher didn't give me enough time."	

8 YEAR OLDS

Physical	Date Observed
Enjoys vigorous activity; likes to dance, roller blade, swim, wrestle, bicycle, fly kites	
Seeks opportunities to participate in team activities and games: soccer, baseball, kickball	
Exhibits significant improvement in agility, balance, speed, and strength	
Copies words and numbers from blackboard with increasing speed and accuracy; has good eye–hand coordination	
Possesses seemingly endless energy	

Cognitive	Date Observed
Collects objects; organizes and displays items according to more complex systems; bargains and trades with friends to obtain additional pieces	
Saves money for small purchases; eagerly develops plans to earn cash for odd jobs; studies catalogues and magazines for items to purchase	
Begins taking an interest in what others think and do; understands there are differences of opinion, cultures, distant countries	
Accepts challenge and responsibility with enthusiasm; delights in being asked to perform tasks at home and in school; interested in being rewarded	
Likes to read and work independently; spends considerable time planning and making lists	
Understands perspective (shadow, distance, shape); drawings reflect more realistic portrayal of objects	
Language	
Delights in telling jokes and riddles	
Understands and carries out multiple-step instructions (up to five steps); may need directions repeated because of not listening to the entire request	
Enjoys writing letters or sending e-mail messages to friends; includes imaginative and detailed descriptions	
Uses language to criticize and compliment others; repeats slang and curse words	
Understands and follows rules of grammar in conversation and written form	
Is intrigued with learning secret word codes and using code language	
Converses fluently with adults; can think and talk about past and future: "What time are we leaving to get to the swim meet next week?"	
Social/Emotional	
Begins forming opinions about moral values and attitudes; declares things right or wrong	
Plays with two or three "best" friends, most often the same age and gender; also enjoys spending some time alone	

Social/Emotional, continued	Date Observed
Seems less critical of own performance but is easily frustrated when unable to complete a task or when the product does not meet expectations	
Enjoys team games and activities; values group membership and acceptance by peers	
Continues to blame others or makes up alibis to explain own shortcomings or mistakes	
Enjoys talking on the telephone with friends	

9 TO 13 YEAR OLDS

Cognitive	Date Observed
Are capable of sustained interest	
Can begin to think logically	
Begin to understand cause and effect	
Understand abstract concepts	
Can apply logic and solve problems	
Can consider more than one solution to problems	
Enjoy problem-solving games and puzzles	

Language	Date Observed
Use language to communicate ideas	
Can use language to express feelings	
Can use abstract words	
Often resort to slang and profanity	
Are often argumentative and contradict adults	

Social/Emotional	Date Observed
Are sensitive to criticism	
Look for friendly relationships with adults	
Make value judgments about their own behavior	
Are aware of the importance of belonging	
Exhibit strong conformation to gender role	
Are independent and self-sufficient	
Begin to develop a moral values system	
May experience stress due to physical changes	
Seek self-identity	

Physical	Date Observed
Have high energy level	
Girls begin adolescent growth spurt	
Boys follow with a growth spurt	
Early maturing is related to positive self-image	
Boys have improved motor development and coordination	
Both boys and girls master skills necessary for playing games	

(Content in this section is adapted from Allen, K. E., & Marotz, L. (2007). Developmental profiles: Pre-birth through twelve, 5th ed. Clifton Park, NY: Delmar.)

QUESTIONS FOR REFLECTION

Every Child is Different

1. In thinking about my knowledge of child development stages and theorists, the one that I am most familiar with is _____, because _____.

   How will this knowledge be used to assess the children I teach?

   In thinking about my knowledge of child development stages and theorists, the one that I am least familiar with is _____, because _____.

   If I don't acquire this knowledge before I am teaching children, what might the consequence be in performing as a competent teacher?

   To prevent this from happening I plan to _____.

2. In thinking about the principles of development, the one that has the most meaning for me is _____.

   I think this is because _____.

   I still don't understand _____.

3. When I think about my own temperament and the modifications that I might need to make in the classroom for children with different temperaments from mine, it makes me think that _____.

4. In thinking about my own social/cultural context, I realize that the most powerful influence in my life has been _____.

The most negative influence in my life has been _____.

I believe I will need to _____ in order to overcome that negative influence. I will begin by _____.

5. In thinking about children with exceptionalities, it makes me think _____.

It makes me feel _____.

I plan to _____.

3

EVERY OBSERVER IS DIFFERENT

Before you begin to look at children, you should take a look at yourself. You view children through a unique lens. You will see (or not see) certain things in children because of who you are, what you know, and how you were raised and taught. Take a look at yourself.

KNOWLEDGE BASE

Knowledge is the base of all wisdom. Some may have knowledge but not the wisdom to use it. Hopefully, along the way, your knowledge of child development will be the foundation on which you build all that you do professionally, with wisdom. It will guide the general development of curriculum and the individualization of that curriculum for specific children. It will guide your classroom practices regarding the environment, scheduling routines and transitions, verbal interactions, and child guidance. It will be the standard against which you measure each child's development and the roadmap to anticipating the next skill or stage of development for each child and group. It will be the screen through which you sift behaviors, bringing to the surface those that may indicate something outside of the expected, demanding a second look. The knowledge of child development is the key to your expertise as a teacher and as an effective observer of children. Several factors have formed your own knowledge base and will influence what you observe and how you interpret it. Here are a few to think about.

NATURAL ABILITIES AND LEARNED SKILLS

You are unique in the abilities and traits you were born with, and what you have learned along the way. These may include abilities such as:

- Attention to detail
- Literacy skills—reading, writing, vocabulary, expressions
- Multitasking
- Attention span
- Patience
- Temperament
- Tolerance

CULTURAL CONTEXT

This is more than whether you are Puerto Rican or Irish (although that may bring with it a set of expectations for behavior). Here are a few components of culture to consider:

- Values—collective ideas about what is right or wrong, good or bad, and desirable or undesirable in a particular culture, serving as broad guidelines for social living
- Beliefs—acceptance or conviction that certain things are true or real
- Customs—actions that are learned as a part of everyday life such as manners, holidays, clothing, male/female behavior
- Inborn and learned characteristics—attitudes and actions that guide behavior such as mannerisms, expressions, self-esteem, self-control
- Child-rearing—attitudes and practices regarding:

    - infants, such as swaddling, spoiling, separate sleeping arrangements
    - toddlers, such as putting away breakable items, handling temper tantrums, toilet training
    - preschoolers, such as level of independence, tolerance for bad language, obedience
    - school-agers, such as expectations for range of freedom, self-care, household responsibilities

PAST EXPERIENCES

This is where you can reflect on what you have learned as "best practice in early childhood" and what you have experienced, and then make a judgment about what to do if there is a contradiction. Explore the reasons for the contradiction, the rationale behind the new idea, and how you will incorporate what you have learned into your own practices as a teacher. Experience will certainly give you knowledge and a practical base from which to work, but it may also instill some ideas and practices that may be inappropriate for you as a professional.

With Children: You may come from a big family, where taking care of younger siblings, cousins, or other relatives has given you a wide range of experience with children. Or you may have experience as parents.

With Programs: You may have worked in the early childhood field for quite a while, so you have observed and gained experience with children of a certain age.

With Families: You may feel qualified and have experience with children, but cringe when it comes to dealing with families. Some people feel intimidated when dealing with adults. You will encounter family members who are demanding, controlling, and seem as if they are mean to their children. You will interact with families of very different cultures from your own, with different values, beliefs, customs, and attitudes towards rearing children. Some family members may already be your friends, or may become very close because of personality or endearing qualities. Understand that these situations may interfere with seeing the child clearly and fairly, so observation methods are selected to try to erase these potential biases.

PRESENT SITUATION

The reality is that all your own past experiences, education, and interactions will be backdrops for what happens to you on any given day that may interfere with your seeing a child objectively.

Personally: We all have good days and bad, health concerns, short- or long-term illnesses, personal traumas, and even little quirks or irritations that affect our mood, attitude, and performance. By having a range of observation tools, a system for collecting data on each child (that has structure but some flexibility), and an awareness of your own present state, you should decide if this is a day for you to *not* do child observation because of intervening factors that might sway the assessment.

Programmatically: On the other hand, you might be constrained in what, how, and when you collect child data because of the program's philosophy and practice. Hopefully you can influence the practices of the program so that they are objective and fair to children. If that is not within your power, then you can make a personal, ethical commitment to augment the required assessments with others that are more objective. You can share those with the family as well, without editorial comment regarding the program's choice.

The whole purpose of learning to use various observation and recording methods is to see each child as an individual, setting aside our own values, beliefs, culture, and to assess the child objectively, without bias.

QUESTIONS FOR REFLECTION

Every Observer Is Different

Think about your own differences that may affect your ability to observe children objectively:

■ Knowledge base

_____

■ Natural and learned skills

_____

■ Cultural context

_____

■ Past experiences

_____

■ Present situation

_____

   ■ Personally

_____

   ■ Programmatically

_____

CHAPTER

4

DIFFERENT WAYS TO WRITE DOWN WHAT WE SEE

"Why different ways? Why not just give them a test?" you might ask. When you know about young children, you know that they grow and change rapidly, can be easily distracted in a testing situation, and have no interest or understanding of performing on demand. Because of this, there are some guiding principles for the selection of assessment tools (NAEYC 2003):

- Used for intended purposes

- Appropriate for age and other characteristics of children being assessed

- In compliance with professional criteria for quality

- Results are used to understand and improve learning

- Evidence is gathered from realistic settings that reflect children's actual performance

- Use multiple sources of information, gathered over time

- Identified concerns are followed up with referral or other intervention

- Use of formal standardized norm-referenced tests is limited

- Staff and families understand the assessment and results

Just as there are many ways to cook a chicken, depending on what you want as a result, there are many ways to write down or record what we've seen depending on what we are looking for. We use the word "record" because the word means to copy or duplicate something else. (A word of caution here, the observer must be *unobtrusive*—anytime you are observing someone closely,

76

the act of being watched may change the behavior of that person so that what you see is not natural. For developmental assessment, that skews the normal behavior and actions we want to see. And another reminder, no matter how important it is to observe and record for all the right reasons, nothing is more important than attending to the safety and other needs (physical, social, emotional) of the children.)

Teachers of young children should learn and practice research-based assessment systems and measures, understanding the advantages and disadvantages of each method, its appropriateness for the age of the child, and moving from informal, play-based assessment to more formal assessments tied to learning objectives and standards. These methods include teacher-generated observations, recorded according to the mandates of the method (checkmarks, written descriptions, dates, tallies, etc.), but also include samples of children's work, and audio, video, and photographic documentation.

● ● ● ● ● ● ● *Think About It* ● ● ● ● ● ● ● ●

Ask yourself these questions:

What do I Want to Know About?	What Kind of Method will Yield that Information?	How will I Gather it?
The family—beyond the demographics	First language, values and beliefs, goals for the child at the program	Questionnaires, interviews, casual conversations
Individual child	Focused methods on one child at a time, looking at each developmental domain: social, emotional, cognitive, creative, physical	At various times throughout the day: arrivals/departures, free choice times, large/small group, routines, interactions with children/adults, reaction to unusual situations
Individual child over time	Focused methods on one child at a time, looking at each developmental domain: social, emotional, cognitive, creative, physical	Repeating observations using similar types of methods at regular intervals
The group	Methods that gather the same kind of information on all the children at the same time	When the whole group is engaged in a similar activity
The program	Methods that evaluate the environment, specific areas, staff or interpersonal relationships	

The types or methods can be categorized into four kinds of results.

DESCRIPTIVE

These methods preserve the details and let the reader or viewer interpret what they mean. This is called "open" recording. Attempts are made to be as accurate and detailed as possible. The reader or viewer should have the feeling of actually having been there and witnessed the event or behavior firsthand.

Anecdotal

An event or selection of the child's behavior is described in objective terms. The description tells the sequence of events beginning with the setting (where it took place), what occurred, and the result. This complete story can be very short but still convey much information. In the example below, you will notice that the descriptive account is written on the left side of the paper. This leaves the right side for "Comments and Conclusions." By using only the left side, the paper can be folded back and given to someone else to read for a second opinion.

EXAMPLE:

9/3/year Hattie (4 yrs, 3 mo.)	Comments/Conclusions
Dramatic Play area—set up as a shoe section of a department Store.	Hattie often plays in the Dramatic Play area, most often alone
H is down on her hands and knees in front of a shelf that has about 25 pair of shoes lined up. She calls back over her shoulder, "I need a pair of black ankle straps. Can anyone help me?" A. comes over and says, "May I help you, Ma'am?" Hattie replies, "You got these in size 4?" A. hands her a pair of red tap shoes and replies, "No, but we have these in size 6." "Sold!" Hattie says and snatches the shoes A. has offered,	Obviously she's been shopping! This is a good way to initiate a play partner to join her. H. often uses grammatical slang in her dramatic play but correct grammar most of the time otherwise. H. is highly dramatic in this play episode, displaying impatience that is uncharacteristic for her.

9/3/year Hattie (4 yrs, 3 mo.)	Comments/Conclusions
sits down on the floor, and puts them on the wrong feet, tying each one in a loose knot. She stands up, taps a bit, smiles, and clomps off to the easel to paint.	Too bad that it didn't evolve into a more interactive play session. I'll try to expand the play to attract another child so the social interaction can be richer. She is satisfied!

DETAILS TO NOTICE: *Every* recording must be dated. Hattie is the "target" child, so her age is included. The notes explain behavior that is unusual, so that the reader does not generalize this behavior as typical. The other child is only identified by initial for confidentiality.

EXERCISE

What can you tell about Hattie from this anecdotal record?

    Experience

    Language

    Physical abilities

    Social interactions

    And the other child?

BAD EXAMPLE: 9/3 Hattie (4 yrs, 3 mo.) was playing shoe store and asked for help. A. gave her a pair that she put on and left.

This is not descriptive, but is general, and just summarizes the action. The specific details, including language style, are lost.

Running/Specimen

The same technique is used as an anecdotal recording, except it is not done for a specific incident or event, but for a block of time, showing a sample of the child's behavior.

EXAMPLE:

9/3/year 9:47 a.m.	Comments/Conclusions
H. (4 yrs, 3 mo.) wearing red tap shoes is at the easel, using left hand, painting single vertical stripes of each color. She is humming a rock tune and bouncing to her own music as she paints. She then makes horizontal lines. Stops humming. Takes a brush in each hand and makes dots in each space. She speeds up, dots, dip, dots, dip, then starts to smear the brushes back and forth. 9:48 H. has covered the whole page, which is now gray. She drops the brushes back into the paint, says, "Done!" and clomps off over to the block area. There are 3 boys building with blocks on the floor. "Whatcha makin?" They look up but don't answer. "I said, 'Whatcha doin', dudes?" F. says, "Bug off, no women allowed here." H. puts her hands on her hips, shifts weight to one side and says, "Can too!" The bell rings for pickup. H. kicks off the red shoes. 9:49 Teacher says, "Hattie, those shoes belong in the shoe department." H. replies, "I ain't no clerk. I the customer." Teacher comes over and pins a round button to her shirt. "Now you are the clerk."	

EXERCISE

What can you tell about Hattie?

    Experience

    Language

    Physical abilities

    Social interactions

    And the other child?

Do you want to know what happened next? In a running or specimen record we have a segment, but we may not know what happened next. The record stops because time was up or something else happened that demanded the recorder's attention. However, details have been captured about the target child.

BAD EXAMPLE: "Hattie painted a design, then didn't like it and mixed the colors together. She tried to play with blocks but the boys wouldn't let her. She refused to pick up the shoes."

This loses the descriptive detail of her painting process, her social interaction and language with the boys in the block area, her creative "excuse" for not picking up, and the teacher's equally wise strategy for encouraging her to do so.

When should you write anecdotal records? Some ideal times when you can focus on one child at a time are:

- Arrival/departures
- Self-help skills—eating, washing, toileting, sleeping
- Free choice time—art, sand/water play, dramatic play, blocks, table games, manipulatives
- Circle time—singing, listening/reading stories
- Outdoors—playtime, planned activities, field trips
- Solitary play
- Social play

- Transitions from one activity to another

- Unusual events or behavior

Media

Photos and audio or video recording are also descriptive ways to record an event or behavior.

PHOTOS: One picture does tell a lot. Hattie at the shoe department, Hattie tying the shoes, Hattie painting at the easel, or Hattie talking in the block area. Photos capture a moment in time; even a series of photos leaves out what happened in between. Of course, the big missing pieces of photos are the movements and language.

EXERCISE

Pull out one of your early childhood textbooks and randomly select a photograph of a child. Don't pay attention to the photo's caption or any text. From just observing the photo, draw some conclusions about the child:

    Age and sex

    Activity

    Mood

    Level of involvement

    Areas of development you see displayed:

        Physical

        Social

        Emotional

        Cognitive

Imagine you are the child's teacher, and you are showing the photograph to a family member at pickup time. What would you say about the photo?

AUDIO RECORDING: If we only heard Hattie's conversations, much would be missing from what we know about her. But if we are only focusing on a child's speech (the sounds, enunciation, articulation) and language (expressions, vocabulary, meaning), an audio recording may be more helpful than a written record, even if the exact words are written phonetically.

EXERCISE

In a public place, listen for the voice of a child. What can you tell about the child by just listening?

VIDEO RECORDING: The above anecdotal or running/specimen records actually seem like a video recording. You could "see" what was happening as you read the record. That's what good descriptive written records do. Video recording captures more details because you really see them; however, a teacher is not a videographer, so notetaking is a better fit with the teacher's busy role in the class-room. Since most children notice that the recording is taking place, it tends to change their behavior.

QUANTITATIVE

There are observation methods that help you count how often an event or behavior occurs. This is a "closed" method because all details of the behavior are not recorded, just the frequency. Any conclusions drawn from closed methods are "inferences"— judgments that are made, perhaps accurately, but are not apparent to the reader based on the limited information that is recorded. The details are lost because only the targeted behaviors are tallied.

Tallies/Frequency Count

To keep track of how many and which children spend free-choice time in a certain area, post a tally sheet on the wall next to each area. Make a check mark on the sheet as you observe children playing/working there. This tells you how often the area is used and by whom, giving information on individual children's choices and patterns.

EXAMPLE

BLOCK AREA WEEK OF OCTOBER 1–6

Child's Name	M	T	W	Th	F
Addie		✓			✓✓
Bruce	✓	✓✓	✓✓✓	✓	
Connor					✓
Deena					✓✓
Elijah	✓✓	✓	✓	✓	
Hattie					

Any frequently occurring behavior, or yes/no type data that would be valuable to measure, can be recorded quickly and efficiently by using an event sample or tally. You may find it useful to know

- Who paints at the easel and how often?

- How many times do children (and who) voluntarily go to the book area to look at books?

- How many times does each child participate in group discussions?

- Who sings at circle time?

- Who follows the movements in large group finger-play actions?

- How many times does each toddler use the toilet by request?

This is also a method of recording a certain behavior that you may be working to reduce through an intervention strategy. To see if it is working, measure the frequency before, during, and after the intervention to evaluate its effectiveness.

● ● ● ● ● ● ● ● *Think About It* ● ● ● ● ● ● ●

- **What do you notice in the block area example? As a teacher, should you do anything about that? What could you do?**

Time Samples

A lengthening attention span is a sequential development of the cognitive domain, so one way to measure a child's cognitive development is to measure his or her attention span. To do so requires that you record how long a child plays/works at a particular task. You may follow a particular child and note start and stop times of activities, or you may periodically (by the clock) note what each child is doing. This will yield information about this specific area of development. Some children move so quickly from one area to another that their names will appear more than once in a time block. In the time it takes for you to write names, the child may have moved to another area.

EXAMPLE

TIME SAMPLE 9/27

AREA	9:25	9:30	9:35	9:40	9:45
Art Easel	Addie	Addie	Addie	Hattie	Connor Elijah
Blocks	Bruce Elijah	Bruce	Bruce Elijah	Bruce	Bruce
Computer		Deena	Connor Deena	Connor Elijah	
Dramatic Play	Hattie Deena	Elijah		Hattie	Hattie Addie
Reading	Connor	Connor		Addie	

Think About It

■ **What conclusions can you make about each child's attention span, interests, playmates?**

   Addie?

   Bruce?

   Connor?

Deena?

Elijah?

Hattie?

Standardized Assessments

These are the main purposes for assessment:

- to support children's learning and instruction

- for communicating with families about the child

- to identify children who may need additional services

- to evaluate a program's effectiveness and accountability to sponsors

Standardized assessments can mean many things. They are called "standardized" because the same procedures for the assessment are followed for each and every individual who is assessed.

A "standardized test" is constructed with the following components:

- based on field-accepted standards

- accompanied by a manual that provides background, instructions for administration, and reporting results

- purpose and age group for which the test was designed

- information on how the test was constructed

- the demographic profile of the norm group—the group on which the test was practiced to develop the scoring system

- criterion or performance level in meeting an established standard

- validity—how the test measures what it intends to measure

- reliability—the test's results are accurate and consistent over time

There are different types of standardized assessments:

	Screening and Diagnostic Tests	Readiness Tests	Achievement Tests	Aptitude Tests
What does the test measure?	Abilities such as motor, perceptual, language, cognitive, social/emotional	Basic knowledge and skills	Learning in a specific subject area	Ability, personality traits
How is it administered	Usually individually	Usually individually	Group	Group
How are the results used?	Identify possible learning or developmental problems	Input into decision of readiness to participate in a particular classroom or level	Normative— compared to another group of children	Predict future performance
Widely used tests	Ages & Stages Questionnaire Peabody Picture Vocabulary Test (ppvt-III) Bayley Scales of Infant Development-R	Gesell School Readiness Test, Lollipop Test	Iowa Test of Basic Skills (ITBS)	WISC-R McCarthy Scales of Children's Abilities

Here are some additional screening and assessment tools commonly used in early childhood. You can get more information about them on the Internet. All are available for purchase.

Ages and Stages Questionnaire, 2nd ed. (ASQ) 1999

AGS Early Screening Profiles (ESP) 1990

Battelle Developmental Inventory (BDI-2) 2005

Bayley Scales of Infant Development 1993

Brigance Inventory of Early Development (IED-II) 2004

Early Screening Inventory (ESI-R) 1997

First Screening Test for Evaluating Preschoolers (FirstSTEP) 1993

Hawaii Early Learning Profile (HELP B-3) 2004

Hawaii Early Learning Profile (HELP for Preschool) 1999

High/Scope Child Observation Record (COR) 2003

The Ounce Scale 2003

Work Sampling System (Preschool 3 & 4) 2004

If you are to administer a standardized test, prescribed directions must be followed exactly. The test manual provides a script that you must follow to give directions and to ask the questions. There may be items in a kit that are used as prompts for questions so you will need to be sure that all items are available and that you have practiced the script. While administering the test, your reactions and comments must remain neutral; you must not give praise, acceptance, or indications of a correct or incorrect answer. The test manual will give guidance about the allowance for second questions or prompts. In order for the results to be valid, the testing protocol must be followed exactly. Performance on the standardized test results in a tally of the correct answers, resulting in a raw score. This is then converted into another kind of score, either matching the expected level of proficiency or a percentile rank when compared to the norm group. Sometimes these are then ranked by grade equivalents.

For these reasons, there has been widespread concern over the use and misuse of standardized tests with young children (see NAEYC Position Statement, 2003). The position against using standardized tests on young children is a strong one, but so is the opposing viewpoint that it depends on the instrument, how it is administered, and the uses of the results (see Issues and Trends for an overview of standardized testing and young children).

For our purposes here, these are mentioned here as one of the ways of quantitative measurement. They are a closed method because they do not include exact details, and only record the ability or inability of the child to perform or answer based on pre-determined criteria.

As an advocate for young children, standardized tests should only be used when the test:

- can be shown to lead to beneficial results
- is a follow-up to extensive observation that indicates developmental lags or concerns

- is administered by a qualified professional with carefully selected tests (preferably more than one)

- does not force the child to separate from parents, which causes undue stress and could negatively affect the results of the test

- consists of a wider range of criteria

- does not carry more weight for decisions about the child than testimony from families and teachers and direct observations of the child in familiar environments

- is not just for measuring the effectiveness of a program, teacher, or school

- is individually administered

- is skill-based rather than verbal or written

- requires little or no preparation

To begin evaluating a standardized assessment for its appropriateness for the children you are working with, first compile information about the assessment answering the following questions. Go back to Chapter 1 and then evaluate the assessment according to those guidelines.

Name and author/s

Standardized norm group:

Age _____ Sex _____ Other _____

___ Screening   ___ Assessment

Reliability:

Validity:

Availability in other languages than English:

Cost:

Designed for: (age range)

Developmental areas covered:

___ Expressive language   ___ Receptive language

___ Auditory perception   ___ Reasoning

___ Gross motor   ___ Fine motor

___ Perceptual-motor   ___ Emotional

___ Social

___ Other

Administration:

Amount of time for administration (___ minutes)

___ Individually   ___ Group

Administered by:

___ Teacher   ___ Parents

___ Specialist   ___ Volunteers/assistants

Training materials available:

Parent input by:

___ Questionnaire   ___ Parent interview

Adapted from: Meisels, S. J., Atkins-Burnett, S. (2005). Developmental Screening in Early Childhood: A Guide, 5e. Washington, DC: National Association for the Education of Young Children.

COMPARATIVE

Comparison methods are not conducted child to child, but rather by comparing the child to a set of criteria against which the observed behavior is measured.

Checklists

Checklists require a yes or no answer, so all the details leading to a particular decision are lost. It is the recorder's inference or judgment that is being written down and the reader has to trust that it is based in fact. Developmental checklists are constructed by professionals who know the sequential stages and milestones (specific skills that occur in *most* children at a certain age). Comparing a child to such a developmental checklist can give information on what skills the child has acquired and what skills are next in the developmental continuum. Returning to the checklist at a later time will give indications of the child's progress. Skills not acquired according to the norm (when most children acquire the skill) can be an indicator that there is a developmental lag.

EXAMPLE				
LITERACY RATING SCALE	**DATE**	**DATE**	**DATE**	**DATE**
Looks at books as self-initiated activity				
Listens as part of a group, tuning out distractions				
Joins in during reading				
Books are favorite toys				
Looks at pages left to right				
Points to print while accurately re-telling from pictures				
"Writes" signs to label constructions				
Sounds out letters in unfamiliar words				
Holds pencil/pen with adult grip, good control				

LITERACY RATING SCALE	DATE	DATE	DATE	DATE
Draws and writes words				
Writes name				
Sounds out words and writes on own				

Rating Scales/Rubrics

Do you ever have trouble answering a simple yes or no question? We need more choices or more descriptions to make an inference or decision about the statement (criteria). A rating scale or rubric gives you more choices along a continuum. It could be:

Listens when a book is being read to the group

Never	Usually	Always

A more descriptive rating scale is called a rubric. It includes possible observed behaviors that might occur in a qualitative sequence toward the desired expectation.

Wiggly, no Attention	Intermittent Attention	Listens in on-on-one Situation	Listens as Part of a Group, Tuning out Distractions

In checklists and rubrics, the observer makes a decision if the observed behavior fits the criteria and makes a checkmark or a date. No further details are recorded. The reader must trust the observer's judgment.

OBSERVATION METHODS COMPARISON CHART

Type	Method	Open/Closed	Especially Good for	Physical	Emotional	Social	Cognitive	Language
Descriptive	Anecdotal	Open	Incidents, selected events	X	X	X	X	X
	Running/ specimen	Open	Glimpse into normal behavior	X	X	X	X	X
	Media, photo, audio/ video record	Open	First person, sight/sound Disadvantages: Time-consuming, difficult not to be biased	X	X	X	X	X
Quantitative	Tallies/frequency count	Closed	Counting activities or frequently occurring behavior	x (inferred)	x (inferred)	x (inferred)	x (inferred)	x (inferred)
	Time sample	Closed	Attention span, free-choice activities, playmates	0	0	x (inferred)	0	0
	Standardized tests	Closed	Measuring against a norm group Disadvantages: Lose the details/proof	x (inferred)	0	0	x (inferred)	x (inferred)
Comparative	Checklist	Closed	Measuring against a criteria, yes/no	X	x (inferred)	X	X	x (inferred)
	Rating scale/rubric	Closed	Measuring against a criteria w/sequential choices Disadvantages: Lose the details/proof, only looking for certain behaviors	X	x (inferred)	X	X	x (inferred)

KEY: Developmental area: X is useful in measuring, x measures but is highly inferential, 0 is not useful in measuring this area

QUESTIONS FOR REFLECTION

Different Ways to Write It Down

1. I'd love to have the time to just sit and observe, and write descriptive anecdotal or running records, but I can't because I'm so involved in caring for the children's needs. I wonder how I can make/take the time.

   Perhaps I could....

   Or maybe I could....

   I think I'll try.....

   I love taking pictures of children and tape recording little conversations, but the minute I pick up the camera or tape or video recorder, they stop acting natural. I wonder how I could obtain a more realistic result.

2. I can see where checkmarks are much easier and faster than descriptive recording. I think it would be important to know how many times.........................

   Once I knew that about individual children, I could then.................

3. A time sample seems to be a good way to gather information on the whole class. I like that method because it can show me...........

4. On the subject of standardized tests for young children, I believe..........

   Perhaps if I knew more about _____, I could understand it better.

   What would I do if I were required by my workplace to observe and record using methods I'm not familiar with?

   _____

   _____

   What would I do if I were required by my workplace to use methods I don't agree with?

   _____

   _____

5. I like the idea of using checklists, rating scales and rubrics because ....

   Once I had that information I could then...................

6. I can see from this section that no one method of documenting what I observe will work for all situations. I think I will need to..............

CHAPTER

5

USES OF DOCUMENTATION FOR THE CHILD

So, now you know the reasons why we collect data on each child, and some different ways of writing down what you observe. This next section will give you some suggestions for how you will use what you have collected.

KNOWING THE CHILD

There is no better way to get to know someone than to watch him or her in a variety of settings and situations. The same is true with a child. By observing the child in the following situations what developmental domains may be revealed?

Situation	Developmental Domains
The child arrives with a family member and says goodbye	
The child circles the room and makes selections of what to do next	
The child moves through routines like eating	
The child moves through routines like sleeping	
The child moves through routines like toileting	
The child moves through routines like cleaning up	

Situation	Developmental Domains
The child interacts with the materials and activities of the classroom	
The child interacts with other children	
The child interacts with adults	
The child has to transition from one activity to another	
The child faces frustration or a problem	
The child faces a new or unusual situation	
The child is able/unable to move from one place to another, walking/running, etc.	
The child is able/unable to hold small objects in his/her hand	
The child is able/unable to make wants/needs known to others through words (above 2 years old)	
The child's speech and language abilities are/are not age-appropriate	
The child is able to sit and look at a book in a one-on-one with an adult	
The child displays hunger	
The child displays tiredness	
The child displays fear	
The child has to go to the bathroom	
The child sees parent or family member arrive for pickup	

Each of these is an opportunity to observe and learn what the child is like, revealing developmental and unique characteristics. This knowledge will assist you in a better understanding of the child, and will guide you in your interactions with and plans for that child within the context of the classroom. Each of these observations calls for the thought processes of "What does this mean?" then "What should I do?" and in the light of what you now know, "What should I write down about this?" "Where should I write it and keep it?" "When do I have time to do that!?"

ASSESSING THE CHILD'S DEVELOPMENT

Because you have knowledge of the stages in child development and what is expected for the age of the children you teach, you will always be informally assessing them in your head as you just did in the previous exercise. You will look at a child and see what she can do, then look at another child and see what he can do. You will judge that one child is more advanced in a particular area, but that another is more advanced in a different area. You also take into consideration their age when making judgments because, other than twins, you will rarely have two children of exactly the same age in the group. So how do you make that judgment? It goes back to your child development knowledge and your experience with children long before you ever became a teacher. You *know* about children of this age.

It is the teacher's responsibility to do more than just have this knowledge in his or her head. All quality early childhood programs require teachers to formally assess children's development. The National Association for the Education of Young Children and the National Association of Early Childhood Specialists in State Departments of Education (2003) have issued a position statement regarding assessment of young children. A portion says:

> The methods used should be developmentally appropriate, culturally and linguistically responsive, tied to children's daily activities, supported by professional development, inclusive of families, and connected to specific, beneficial purposes:
>
> (1) making sound decisions about teaching and learning,
>
> (2) identifying significant concerns that may require focused interventions for individual children, and
>
> (3) helping programs improve their educational and developmental interventions.

The application of these principles guide our expectations and practices:

Developmentally appropriate	It should fit the age of the child. We wouldn't expect toddlers to sit down and fill in answers on a bubble sheet.
Culturally and linguistically responsive	We would take into consideration the home language of the child when assessing the child's ability to follow directions for example. We wouldn't expect that items on an assessment would be disrespectful to any child's culture.
Tied to children's daily activities	We would use the natural environment of the classroom during which children are performing their daily routines as the setting for assessment. We wouldn't take the child in a separate room to observe or expect the child to perform tasks on command.
Supported by professional development	The staff expected to assess children's development will be trained to use effective, efficient methods, and supplied with materials and the time to conduct the assessment.
Inclusive of families	Families would also have some input into assessing their own children's development. This recognizes the family as the authority on the child.
Connected to specific, beneficial purposes	This means that there are legitimate uses for the assessments that will benefit the child, such as (1) Helping the teacher plan lessons and activities that will be at the child's level to help him find success, and that are just challenging enough to help the child attain the next step in the sequence of skills and behaviors. (2) When closely observing the child, concerns are raised about expected skills and behaviors that are not present, and further evaluation is done to decide if intervention is needed. (3) When interventions are indicated, the program makes the necessary modifications to meet the developing needs of the child.

The early childhood field advocates assessment by observing and recording using a variety of methods that are best suited for different kinds of results, that are geared to the age and stage of the children's development, and that are repeated over a period of time. You now have some ideas about what that assessment looks like. The next sections will guide your thinking about how you can use those written records to benefit the child and to achieve the outcomes you want as a teacher.

The Code of Ethical Conduct and Statement of Commitment (NAEYC 2005) reminds teachers of the ideals and principles of ethical responsibilities to children:

Ideal 1.6—To use assessment instruments and strategies that are appropriate for the children to be assessed, that are used only for the purposes for which they were designed, and that have the potential to benefit children.

Ideal 1.7—To use assessment information to understand and support children's development and learning, to support instruction, and to identify children who may need additional services.

Principle 1.5—We shall use appropriate assessment systems, which include multiple sources of information, to provide information on children's learning and development.

PLANNING CURRICULUM FOR GROUPS AND INDIVIDUALS

Curriculum is the word we use for what the teacher plans for the group and the individual child. This is based on many factors:

Age/stage of the children: Here we go, back to child development again. When you plan a party for 10-year-olds, the themes, games, and even the food is different from what you would plan for 16 year olds or 40 year olds. When you know the characteristics of *most* children of a certain age, it gives you clues as to what they are capable of and what kinds of activities interest them. When you are the teacher of a group responsible for planning curriculum, you begin planning curriculum based on your general knowledge of child development.

EXERCISE

If you are a teacher of toddlers, think about curriculum planning in the following way:

Most toddlers can walk, run, and climb	So I will make sure that I have equipment in the room for them to....
A characteristic of toddlers is that they love to fill and dump things	I will have....
But another characteristic of toddlers is that they are still putting things in their mouth to explore them and chew on them	I will make sure that I have things for them to fill and dump, including.....
Toddlers love music and love to sing and dance	I will plan each day to include....
Toddlers like to listen to books being read that are....	I will select books that....
Toddlers can't sit still in a group to listen to those books I select	I will plan each day to....
Toddlers can't share toys yet	I will have....
Toddlers are just beginning to use paint, glue, markers, and drawing materials	I won't expect... but will give them the opportunity to....
Toddlers are learning the names of objects and still developing language skills	I will....
Some people call them "terrible" because they may get out of control emotionally, with temper tantrums and aggressive acts towards things and people	I will be extra watchful when... so no one gets hurt.
Toddlers are still taking naps	I will plan....
Toddlers are learning about the world around them, including home, everyday objects, store, doctor, friends, animals	I will plan....

From thinking about the characteristics of most toddlers, the teacher can plan the class-room environment, furnishings, play materials, books, activities, schedule, and some themes or curriculum areas on which to base activities that reinforce what the toddlers know, but give them practice in the physical, creative, cognitive, literacy, language, social, and emotional developmental areas.

Individual children in the group: The curriculum you plan begins with a framework of what most children of this age can do and then becomes more refined as you get to know each child better. You do this by observing, taking notes, and assessing where each child is compared to pre-determined goals and objectives. You learn about children's interests and experiences by talking with them and knowing what is happening in their lives, school, and community. All of this is a lot to remember and that's where note taking (recording) comes in.

Once you know these things about children of this age, and the children in your group in particular, then this will guide the daily activities you plan. Curriculum is planned for the whole group, but can be individualized for a specific child—when you know the child needs a little more practice in one area, is especially interested in something, or has mastered a skill and is ready for a challenge. For infants and toddlers, observations about children's growth and development guide the teacher in making changes in the environment, interactions, and planned experiences. As the children engage in the planned activities, the teacher again observes and records to document how each one reaches the objective of the activity. This measures the child's skills in the developmental area and the effectiveness of the planned activity, and gives indicators of what new ideas can be added to extend

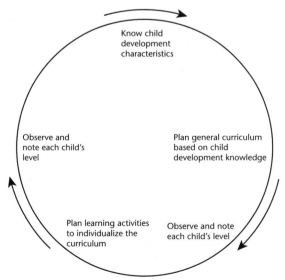

Cycle of observe, plan, observe.

the activity to another learning level. From this, teachers develop short- and long-range plans for the group and individual children. For school-age children, assessments provide information on skill level in content areas such as literacy, mathematics, and science, which teaching approaches are working, and in what areas individual children are having difficulty or need increasing challenges.

From this you can see that it is a cycle.

Social and cultural contexts in which the children live: As *you* get to know the group and the individual children, *your knowledge about the immediate world in which they live and operate will* influence *your* curriculum planning. Children may live in affluence or poverty, in **urban** high-rise apartments or rural areas, in areas where it snows in the winter or is warm year-round, *or near the* ocean, prominent rivers or mountains, or wide-open plains. Children live in the present. Their world usually is quite small, limited to their neighborhood, *and* experiences with family and a limited number of other people quite like themselves. The teacher's knowledge of this social context will help **him or her** understand the child better, have realistic expectations for their knowledge and interests, and plan curriculum that is meaningful and relevant. Of course, because of media and the ease of travel for many families, children's knowledge may be much broader than their own neighborhoods. The teacher's knowledge of that aspect of the children in the group will also enter into assessment and curriculum planning.

The cultural context is another important factor in knowing children. In today's world of diversity, in any one group of children there may be many races, home languages, religions, family constellations, and ethnic cultures. These may affect the child's development and experiences. The observant teacher learns these things about the children in the group, and makes sure that these factors form a lens through which the child is viewed and assessed and in how the curriculum is planned. An understanding of the child's culture is vitally important in planning curriculum that replays familiar themes in the child's world as well as not offending or countering the families' beliefs and practices. Even if all the children in the group are of the same homogeneous group, teachers have a responsibility to prepare all children for a world made up of different kinds of people by including materials, books, and pictures that present images of children of different cultures. Here are four anti-bias goals:

(1) Nurture each child's construction of a knowledgeable, confident self-concept and group identity.

(2) Promote each child's comfortable, empathic interaction with people from diverse backgrounds.

(3) Foster each child's critical thinking about bias.

(4) Cultivate each child's ability to stand up for her/himself and for others in the face of bias.

From Derman-Sparks, & L. Ramsey, P. (2006). *What if all the kids are white*? New York: Teachers College Press.

EXERCISE

We return to the exercise you did earlier about observing children during various times or events in the day. Select an age group (infants, toddlers, preschoolers, or school-agers) and think about one curriculum activity you would plan that fits the developmental level of the age and specific needs of this child:

SITUATION—Select one observable behavior	Plan a curriculum activity for the group or this child based on your observation
The child arrives with a family member and says goodbye	
The child circles the room and makes selections of what to do next	
The child moves through routines like eating	
The child moves through routines like sleeping	
The child moves through routines like toileting	
The child moves through routines like cleaning up	
The child interacts with the materials and activities of the classroom	
The child interacts with other children	

The child interacts with adults
The child has to transition from one activity to another
The child faces frustration or a problem
The child faces a new or unusual situation
The child is able/unable to move from one place to another, walking/running, etc.
The child is able/unable to hold small objects in his/her hand
The child's ability to make wants/needs known to others through words (above 2 years)
The child's speech and language abilities are/are not age-appropriate
The child is able to sit and look at a book in a one-on-one with an adult
The child displays hunger
The child displays tiredness
The child displays fear
The child has to go to the bathroom
The child sees parent or family member arrive for pickup

Philosophy of the program: Curriculum philosophy and planning is often not the sole responsibility of the individual teacher but a collective decision that is made by the staff, the director, or the program owner/sponsor. The philosophy of the program influences the physical environment of the classroom in regards to furnishings, materials such as toys and equipment, supplies, schedule, type of curriculum, any necessary advance planning, and the assessment/evaluation of the children in the group. Because these factors are all related to the philosophy of the program, it is impossible to talk about observation/assessment/evaluation without taking the philosophy into consideration. Here are some of the most widely used curriculum-planning approaches and their implications for observation:

Themes: Teachers design learning activities in various areas including art, large muscle, dramatic play, music and movement, story, and manipulatives. These activities all relate to a theme that has been broken down into subtopics. One example is "Homes"—with separate days or weeks devoted to "My Home," "Farm Animal Homes," "Forest Animal Homes," "Jungle Animal Homes," "Insect Homes," and "Vehicle Homes." The advantage of this kind of planning is that it is based on the children's life experiences, about which they have prior knowledge. It plans for meaningful activities that are related to one another, building and expanding knowledge by bridging between domains. It provides children with different ways to experience and express what they know and have learned about the topic. Assessing various areas of development can be built into the curriculum based on the objective of each of the activities.

The disadvantages of this kind of curriculum are that it is decided by adults and may not be of interest to children, it may not be relevant to their particular experiences or culture, and it may not make the same connections in the child's mind as it does in the adults, because children think differently than adults. It may also leave little room for spontaneity; if a teacher has a plan for a specific day, he or she may not include what is happening currently in the classroom. For example, the day's theme may be insect homes, and the plan is to start an ant farm, watch ants under a microscope, sing songs and move like ants, read a story about ants, and have children work with creative materials and draw their concept of ants. However, three trucks of large equipment arrive that day at the lot across from the classroom, and the workmen start digging the foundation for a building. Unfortunately, that doesn't match the ant theme!

Purchased curriculum: There are hundreds, probably thousands, of companies developing curriculum that are declared to be "developmentally appropriate" for certain ages of children. This curriculum may be comprehensive, and include all the developmental domains, have an accompanying development assessment piece, and, of course, be easier for the teachers.

However, the curriculum writers do not have knowledge of the children in your group, so it may not be appropriate in all the ways we have mentioned earlier.

Emergent curriculum: The adults (including families) and children discover interests and decide to investigate questions that arise. The teacher then plans activities that will help uncover and construct new understandings of subjects relevant to the children. An activity can come from an event in a child's life that is shared with and captures the interest of the group, such as attending a wedding or having a new baby. It can come from the interests or passions of the adults, for example the teacher's interest in bee hives and honey or a family's pizza-making business. Upon exploration of the subject, children ask various questions and then discuss how to find the answers. The example of the large trucks arriving to dig a foundation for a house mentioned earlier may capture the children's interest, and inspire a host of questions and observations about the sequence of building construction as it evolves right outside the window of their classroom. The teacher's role is not only to try to elicit meaningful questions, but to facilitate the building of knowledge through classroom experiences that will also inform the teacher of developmental objectives. Obviously, emergent curriculum is most appropriate for older preschoolers and younger school-age children.

Disadvantages of emergent curriculum include the misconception that the teacher does not plan, but rather sits back and lets it happen. On the contrary, emergent curriculum requires a teacher who is experienced in facilitating learning in this way, a strong background in child development, and a repertoire of learning strategies to meet the learning objectives. It is not a comfortable fit for a teacher whose personal style is organized and predictable. Emergent curriculum can evolve into a highly teacher-directed approach that may counteract the purpose of following the children's interests. Observing the children's attention and continued interest closely will prevent this from happening. It may be somewhat more difficult to connect the curriculum directly to learning standards, but the teacher who uses observation as authentic assessment can show through data gathered that indeed, learning standards have been met while using this method of curriculum planning.

Each of these methods of curriculum planning may use observation and assessment to inform the development of meaningful, relevant, and developmentally and culturally appropriate learning experiences.

Values, beliefs, and learning/teaching style of the teacher: When he or she has the responsibility and freedom to plan, the teacher's own values, beliefs, and style affect the curriculum. As always, when we observe children, it is through our own frame of reference, through a lens that is colored by our own upbringing, social and cultural context, and learning style. This is where self-reflection comes in, as we must constantly look inward and think about what we have observed and its meaning, not only regarding the child's development but our own reactions to it.

MEASURING PROGRESS OVER TIME

Observing and writing down what we have observed regarding a child's development is not a one-time event. While it has value for all the reasons already discussed (knowing the child, assessing the child's development against a standard measure, and planning curriculum), it is by seeing children's progress as they grow and learn that we really can measure what is happening. In every living organism, change indicates the progress of life. In children, the changes that take place in the first year are the most dramatic, as they progress from totally dependent to a mobile, expressive individual. The changes that take place in the next several years are profound and easily identified; they grow, speak, move, and think. Growth and development slow, but there are still milestones along the way that indicate that the individual is maturing according to the predictable sequence. Because change happens so rapidly in the first years, more frequent measurement is needed. Of course, daily notations are made about the infant's intake, diaper changes, eating, and sleeping. Notations are made of toddlers, preschoolers, and school-age children whenever something eventful happens that we want to remember. (We remember whatever we write down!) What we are talking about here is regular, systematic developmental assessment. That does not occur in the teacher's busy day without planning, planning what it is we want to observe, having the right materials available, and making the time to do it.

How often we measure progress depends on the age of the child. A number of development checklists can be used, as well as those methods that gather open data and preserve the details of the observation, such as anecdotal and running records. There is much to be seen and recorded, so it is important to have an observation planning system or calendar set up to remind you to observe and record. It is more manageable if you spread the observations out over the month and year so that you are not trying to do all your observing on the eve of the next month or observation period. The chart below may help you decide how often to observe. If you write reminders on a calendar of the developmental area you wish to observe and document each month and each week, it will help you spread the work out throughout the month, and make sure that you record information on each child in each developmental area often enough to measure change.

OBSERVATION FREQUENCY CHART

	Physical	Social	Emotional	Language	Literacy	Intellectual	Creative
Infants	Monthly First wk of every month	Every other month Second wk of months 2, 4, 6, 8, 10	Every other month Second wk of months 1, 3, 5, 7, 8, 11	After 6 months, monthly 3rd wk of month	After 6 months, every other month 3rd wk of months 2, 4, 6, 7, 10		Curiosity, after 6 months 4th wk of month
Toddlers	Every other month First wk of every month	Every other month Second wk of months 2, 4, 6, 8, 10	Every other month Second wk of months 1, 3, 5, 7, 8, 11	Every other month 3rd wk of months 1, 3, 5, 7, 9, 11	Every other month 3rd wk of months 2, 4, 6, 7, 10	Every other month	Every other month 4th wk of months 2, 4, 6, 8, 10
Preschoolers	Every 3 months First wk of months 1, 4, 7, 10	Every 3 months First wk of months 2, 5, 8, 11	Every 3 months First wk of months 3, 6, 9, 12	Every 3 months 3rd wk of months 1, 4, 7, 10	Every 3 months 3rd wk of months 3, 6, 9, 12	Every 3 months 3rd wk of months 2, 5, 8, 11	Every 3 months 4th wk of months 3, 6, 9, 12
School Age	Every 4 months First wk of months 1, 5, 9	Every 4 months First wk of months 2, 6, 10	Every 4 months First wk of months 3, 7, 9	Every 4 months 3rd wk of months 1, 5, 9	Every 4 months 3rd wk of months 3, 7, 11	Every 4 months 3rd wk of months 2, 6, 10	Every 4 months 4th wk of months 3, 7, 11

It is important to observe and record in all developmental levels for *every* child in the group. If left to chance, the "interesting" or "difficult" children have many recorded observations and the quiet, less troublesome children have fewer.

IDENTIFYING SPECIAL NEEDS

When a child's development is drastically different from typical patterns and sequences, it is called "atypical." It may be atypical in only one area, such as language, or in several developmental areas. The child may be experiencing delays or just slower than normal development, but still be progressing according to the normal pattern. It may be a developmental area that is arrested, has stopped developing, or that was never present or progressing at all. These will be more profound disabilities. It has been estimated that 17 percent of children in the United States have a developmental or behavioral disability. Early identification and intervention is mandated by the Individuals with Disabilities Education Act (IDEA), which requires states to provide early identification and provision of services to (1) infants and toddlers with developmental delays, (2) infants and toddlers with established conditions associated with delays, and (3) (at the state's option) children at risk for delays. As the early childhood teacher, you are often one of the first to observe and suspect a delay. It is not for you to identify or diagnose this, but to document and refer the family to their medical provider for further evaluation.

Public Law 105–17, the Individuals with Disabilities Education Act amendments of 1997, gives guidelines regarding child assessments:

■ A variety of culturally and linguistically fair assessment tools and strategies should be used. No single procedure can be the sole criterion for decisions regarding intervention.

■ Assessment tools and strategies should provide information that directly assists in determining the educational needs of the child, linking evaluation, placement, and educational programming.

■ Information from all sources must be documented and carefully considered. This includes:

● Evaluation information provided by the parent

- Current classroom-based assessments and observations

- Observation by teachers and related service providers

- Classroom data from the cognitive, physical, behavioral, and developmental domains must be gathered and used to make program decisions, monitor student performance, and help the staff provide both general and educational services.

These guidelines are applicable to all child assessments.

Infant and toddler screenings focus on health needs and acquisition of developmental milestones. These are typically done by health care providers, but are also the responsibility of the teacher. Teachers' assessments of preschoolers and school-age children continue to observe growth and development, but learning difficulties may give indications that there are physical or developmental problems that should be addressed. When observing children through the knowledge base of typically developing behaviors, and a delay, unusual behavior, or lack of skill is observed, that is called a "red flag." It is an alert, a signal that further observations and evaluations should be done to determine the extent and possible cause, and if an intervention can be applied to help overcome the deficit or delay. Remember that you may be seeing the child on a "bad day," so if what you have observed raises concern, wait a few days and observe again. Every child is different, and is growing and developing at different rates—even at different rates in various developmental areas. If you are observing infants and toddlers who were born prematurely, you should judge their developmental age full-term age rather than actual birth date.

DEVELOPMENTAL ALERTS

These are intended not as a screening tool but to give guidance of what may be indicators of concern.

(There are similar developmental alerts in the Developmental Milestones by Age chart on page 35. Use both lists to help you determine if there is cause for concern.)

Observe carefully and often and confer with on-staff developmental experts. Use caution when you ask the family if they have seen this skill, action, or behavior. This is a very sensitive area and must be approached with tact, understanding, and empathy.

By 3 months, the child should:

- Lift head and turn it from side to side
- Follow with eyes a moving object or person
- Grasp an object
- Wiggle and kick arms and legs
- Make cooing, gurgling sounds
- Smile
- Communicate hunger, fear, discomfort
- React to peek-a-boo games

By 6 months, the child should:

- Hold head steady
- Reach for and grasp objects
- Move toys from one hand to another
- Shake, explore, and put toys in mouth
- Sit with only a little support
- Roll over
- Imitate familiar actions
- Babble
- Know familiar faces
- Laugh and squeal with happiness, scream if annoyed
- Smile at self in mirror

By 12 months, the child should:

- Drink from cup with help
- Feed self finger food
- Grasp small objects with thumb and index finger
- Put small blocks in and out of container
- Crawl on hands and knees
- Pull up and stand alone
- Walk with one hand being held

- Copy sounds and actions
- Look for an object hidden out of sight
- Say first words
- Recognize family members' names
- Show affection to familiar adults
- Show apprehension about strangers
- Raise arms to be picked up
- Understand simple commands

By 18 months, the child should:

- Walk without help
- Run stiffly with eyes on ground
- Turn pages in a book
- Stack two blocks
- Identify an object in a picture book by pointing when object is named
- Laugh at silly actions
- Follow simple, one-step directions
- Say eight to ten words you can understand
- As specifically for mother or father
- Use "hi," "bye"
- Ask for something by pointing or using one word
- Become anxious when separated from parent(s)
- Play alone on the floor with toys
- Seem selfish at times

By 2 years, the child should:

- Feed self with spoon
- Stack three to four blocks
- Toss or roll a large ball
- Bend over to pick up a toy and not fall

- Go down steps backward, crawling

- Point to five to six body parts when asked

- Have a vocabulary of several hundred words

- Use two- to three-word sentences

- Sometimes get angry and have temper tantrums

- Treat a doll or stuffed animal as though it were alive

- Refer to self by name and use "me" and "mine"

- Verbalize desires and feelings, "I want…"

By 3 years, the child should:

- Feed self with some spilling

- Hold a crayon well

- Wash and dry hands by self

- Build a tower of four to five blocks

- Dress self with help

- Use the toilet with some help

- Walk up stairs with alternating feet

- Walk on a straight line

- Pedal a tricycle

- Recognize sounds in the environment

- Remember what happened yesterday

- Know what is and is not food

- Count aloud but not always in right order

- Look through a book alone

- Match objects (circles/squares, picture to object, things that go together)

- Use three- to five-word sentences

- Repeat simple rhymes

- Name at least one color correctly

- Try to make others laugh

- Know first and last name
- Play spontaneously with two to three children in a group

By 4 years, the child should:

- Feed self with little spilling
- Try to write name
- Draw a circle, face
- Try to cut, button, buckle
- Build a tower of seven to nine blocks
- Use the toilet alone
- Catch a bouncing ball
- Walk downstairs using rail and alternating feet
- Recognize red, yellow, and blue
- Understand big, little, tall, short
- Sort by shape or color
- Count up to five objects
- Follow three instructions given at one time
- Have a large vocabulary and speak clearly
- Use good grammar most of the time
- Want explanations
- Ask questions
- Separate from parent for a short time without crying
- Pretend to play with imaginary objects
- Sometimes cooperate and share with other children
- Like to act independently
- Know age and city/town

Children 6 through 12 years old should:

- Exercise growing independence
- Have several friends that may change from day to day
- Define self by appearance, possessions, and activities

- Resolve conflict through negotiation

- Practice inner control

- Seek approval of others, first family then friends

- Develop coordination toward adult levels

- Differentiate between "good" and "bad" choices and demonstrate conscience

- Read and write at or near grade level

QUESTIONS FOR REFLECTION

Uses of Documentation for the Child

1. I understand that by focusing my observations on an individual child, I can know the child much better but _____.

2. The whole idea of assessment is one that makes me feel _____ because _____. Perhaps _____.

3. I thought curriculum planning was when the teacher _____. Using observation to plan curriculum for a child or the group seems _____. I will need to _____.

4. It will be gratifying to look back on earlier observations to see a child's progress. That will make me feel _____ and make me want to _____. In order to do this I will need to _____.

5. When I see a developmental lag, I will _____. It will be difficult to _____. One of the things I will be sure to do is _____.

6

SHARING DOCUMENTATION

The primary purpose of observing and documenting what we see is to help advance the child's learning and development in the classroom. We know the child, assess development, use that assessment to make sure that the curriculum in general is useful for all the children, and individualize the curriculum in specific areas for certain children. We measure developmental progress by returning to our documentation several times during the year and expect to see improvements and progress. If our documentation does not show progress, or if it gives indicators of developmental lags, we take action. There are other uses for our authentic assessments. It also is of interest to others beyond the classroom. This section discusses that sharing.

COMMUNICATION WITH FAMILIES

Teachers begin their knowledge of the child by obtaining information from the family, then sharing what they learn about the child in the classroom through clear, respectful, and constructive communications. All of our documentation on a child should be accessible to that child's family (except if there is a suspicion of child abuse; more about that later). Some types of information sharing include:

- Infants and toddlers—teachers and families share information about the child's health, daily routines, and progress along the development continuum.

- Preschoolers—sharing information periodically helps make decisions regarding children's learning goals and approaches to learning.

■ School-age children—this information is more likely to be shared through letter or numerical grades, but should include narrative comments and examples of children's work that demonstrate how the grade is formulated.

When large-scale assessments are used, the teacher should inform the family of their meaning, their uses, and any limitations of the results (NAEYC 2003).

There are several organizations that have issued standards of practice for sharing observations and assessments with families:

NAEYC *Early Childhood Program Standards and Accreditation Criteria* (2005)

Standard 2.047—Parent Conferences: Along with short informal daily conversations between parents and care-givers, planned communication shall be scheduled with at least one parent of every child in care:

■ To review the child's development and adjust-ment to care

■ To reach agreement on appropriate, non-violent, disciplinary measures

■ To discuss the child's strengths, specific health issues, and concerns such as persistent behavior problems, developmental delays, special needs, overweight, underweight, or eating or sleeping problems.

American Academy of Pediatrics, Caring for Our Children: National Health and Safety

Performance Standards: Guidelines for Out-of-Home Child Care Programs, 2nd ed. (2002)

Standard 2.047 Parent conferences shall be scheduled with at least one parent of every child in care:

(a) To review the child's development and adjust-ment to care

(b) To reach agreement on appropriate, nonviolent, disciplinary measures;

(c) To discuss the child's strengths, specific health issues and concerns such as persistent behavior problems, developmental delays, special needs, overweight, underweight, or eating or sleeping problems

National Association of Family Child Care Accreditation

Standard 1.18—The provider discusses concerns with parents when they arise and tries to reach a mutually satisfying solution.

The Code of Ethical Conduct and Statement of Commitment (NAEYC 2005) states that ethical responsibilities to families are:

Ideal 2.7—To share information about each child's education and development with families and to help them understand and appreciate the current knowledge base of the early childhood profession.

Principle 2.7—We shall inform families about the nature and purpose of the program's child assessments and how data about their child will be used.

It is only common sense that we would share what we learn about children in our group with the people who have the most interest in those children—their families. However, that is possibly one of the most difficult and sensitive tasks. Sometimes what the teacher thinks is cute and funny, the family finds offensive, rude, a poor reflection on their parenting, or a lack of manners or intelligence. Sometimes even a hint that the child is not developing normally will cause the family to feel angry, afraid, defensive, or depressed. Before the teacher discusses any concerns over development or behavior, he or she must establish a comfortable line of communication with the family. It starts with the initial contact, when the child and parent visit the classroom. In some programs, the relationship may begin even earlier, when the teacher visits the child at home. This is an opportunity for the teacher to see the child in the context of the home environment, not as an inspection of the house, but as a way of better understanding the child and the family. Wherever the first meeting takes place, the teacher sets the tone of respect and openness, and demonstrates the recognition of the family as the authorities in knowledge about the child. The teacher will simply be adding another dimension to that knowledge.

DAILY COMMUNICATION: In a child care program, you will greet the child and the family member who brings the child in. At that time, a friendly greeting of welcome and a smile start the day off right for everyone. Add a bit of social exchange, personalized with news and information about the child. The program may have a system of daily intake that includes a form where information can be written, such as how the child slept the night before, how the child is feeling, any changes or concerns that the staff should know about, and who will be picking the child up at the end of the day. At the end of the day, there is an opportunity for face-to-face communication with the family member or person authorized to take the child home. This too should be a friendly exchange in general terms about the day, forecasts of the next day's activities, and a statement about looking forward to seeing the child again.

The end of the day is not the time to exchange developmental information, behavior issues, or concerns. The parent is tired, you may be tired as well, the child is present, and other parents and children may be around you. Give the parent the information he or she needs, such as the child's eating, sleeping, and toileting data, but do not share negative information. When teachers list the misdemeanors of the day to the parent at the door, it is a form of tattling. It indicates that the teacher (and the child) was out of control, not competent to handle the situation, and hints that the parents can do something about the behavior. They cannot. Try to refrain from this kind of negative communication. It does not help the teacher/parent relationship and does little to solve any difficulties the child may be having.

WRITTEN COMMUNICATION: Often the staff person who sees the child and family member at arrival time may not be the same person who sees them at the end of the day. If children arrive on the bus, family members are seldom seen face-to-face. In these cases, written communication is a must for keeping in touch and exchanging vital information about the child. The same information mentioned above can be exchanged with the family in a written format. It should be factual, friendly, non-accusatory, and positive.

It can be thought of as a "happy note," giving details of the day's or week's events, without a rehearsal of the mistaken or unacceptable behavior that you had to handle with that child.

EXERCISE

Remember the chart that you filled in that asked what you could observe about a child during routines? Go back to it, and select one of the positive words or phrases you wrote in the right-hand column. Now practice writing a factual, positive note to the family about this observation.

SITUATION—Select one observable behavior that you made notes about earlier.	Write a note to send home because the child arrives on a bus, or you don't see the family member at the end of the day.
The child arrives with a family member and says goodbye	
The child circles the room and makes selections of what to do next	
The child moves through routines like eating	
The child moves through routines like sleeping	
The child moves through routines like toileting	
The child moves through routines like cleaning up	
The child interacts with the materials and activities of the classroom	
The child interacts with other children	
The child interacts with adults	
The child has to transition from one activity to another	
The child faces frustration or a problem	
The child faces a new or unusual situation	
The child is able/unable to move from one place to another, walking/running, etc.	
The child is able/unable to hold small objects in his/her hand	

The child is able/unable to make wants/ needs known to others through words (above 2 years old)
The child's speech and language abilities are/are not age-appropriate
The child is able to sit and look at a book in a one-on-one with an adult
The child displays hunger
The child displays tiredness
The child displays fear
The child has to go to the bathroom
The child sees parent or family member arrive for pickup

Keeping in touch with the family through phone calls or e-mails is another way to keep the lines of communication open, showing that you know about the child at school while they know about the child at home and out in the community.

Keep it positive. The same concept of keeping verbal communications positive holds true with written communication, and even more so. Written communication is permanent. It can be misinterpreted. It can be examined for hidden meanings.

Think About It

■ **See what you think of these "friendly" notes. Examine them closely for possible biases or hidden meanings.**

"Suzie is such a cute little thing."

"Rob is a real tough guy. Even when he's hurt he doesn't cry."

"Alexis had a hard day today so she's coming home with a lollipop."

"Daniel had a great time in the dramatic play area today. He especially liked wearing the dress and high heels."

"Anthony will be ready for an early bedtime tonight. He played especially hard outside today."

"Please don't forget to send in more diapers. We've been without them for several days now."

"Please read to Shane every night. He loves stories and it would help him with his vocabulary."

"Corey only cried for a little while after Grandma left her this morning."

"We've noticed that Brenda doesn't smile as much as she did. Is something going on at home that is bothering her? Can we help?"

"We are having a class for families on dealing with difficult behavior and we'd love to see you attend."

FAMILY CONFERENCE: The standards and good professional practice indicate that you should sit down with the family at times throughout the year to discuss the child's progress. This is where your written observations come into play. You are not just talking from your recollections, you have hard data to show that you have been carefully observing, documenting, assessing, and individualizing the curriculum with learning activities to help their child progress in skills and development. Using that file folder or portfolio will give you both points of reference from which to have a meaningful discussion. You may want to have a written report with notations in each developmental area with references to the documentation that supports your findings. It could serve as an outline for your conference.

- Adjustment to school/classroom routines

- Self-help skills

- Physical development—large and small muscles

- Social development

- Emotional development

- Speech and language

- Memory and attention span

- Literacy development

- Math and science knowledge

- Creative arts and dramatic play

- Overall strengths

- Areas we are working on

You notice that the outline includes a strengths area, but not a corresponding "weakness" area. Talk about those areas where the child will develop next, and explain that you are planning certain activities and experiences to help the child make further gains in this area. Your family conference, like every other interaction with the family, starts with social conversation about the weather, the news, big events at the school. The setting is comfortable, with no physical barriers between you and the family. It's best not to sit behind a desk or across the table, as physical barriers are psychological barriers. You are "both on the same side" of the child, the table, or the desk.

Keep your comments positive, and back them up with your documentation. Talk about the child's strengths and the things you are working on. If there is an area of concern, use your documentation to show any indicators that further study is warranted, to benefit both you and the family. Or you may judge that the family is prepared for information regarding a referral. Be cautious of this; it may seem that they are ready, but later you may find that they are questioning your ability to assess and evaluate. It is wise to go slowly, so unless there is a pressing need for immediate action, allow the family to see the area of concern for themselves and decide on a path of action that best suits them. Have a list of referral agencies on hand, but try not to push this until the family asks for it.

It is the documentation that points the way. Use it not to pile up evidence, but to present a fair and accurate picture of the child's development as a whole, stressing the positive areas and problem solving for those areas that seem to need attention. End the conference by stating your appreciation of their attendance and attention, and commending them for the work they have done thus far in rearing their child.

REPORTING/ACCOUNTABILITY TO MEET STANDARDS

Another reason for documenting children's development is to show the teacher's competence as a part of determining the program's effectiveness. While there is a nationwide movement to hold teachers accountable for children's pass/fail rates in public school settings, there is a similar initiative in early childhood programs to show teacher effectiveness. National standards have been developed by nearly every professional organization that examines the key elements that children should know and be able to do at various ages. These standards are measurements against which curriculum and programs can be measured for effectiveness. (See the Internet resources in this book for a list of content areas and Web sites that explore standards.)

EXERCISE: STANDARD SCAVENGER HUNT

(using the RESOURCES—INTERNET in this book)

find the standard for early childhood:

Art

English as a Second Language

Mathematics

Social Studies

National standards have been developed by the U.S. Department of Health and Human Services that oversees the federal Head Start and Early Start programs. Program accreditations such as the National Association for the Education of Young Children and National Association of Family Child Care include aspects of the documentation of children's progress as indicators of quality programs. The purpose of program assessment is not only to affirm that the program is meeting its goals, but to raise awareness of areas where improvements need to be made.

While the teacher has part of the responsibility for the child's development, that part can be a determining factor in helping the child reach his or her full potential in learning and growing. Teachers owe the families periodic reports on their children's progress (more about that in the next section), and must also report the progress that children are making in the program to administrators, who in turn report to sponsors or funding agencies. This kind of reporting is not gathered on the individual child, but is the aggregate or numerical data from standardized measures of performance. This does not necessarily mean a test! It can be the percentage of children who were "on target" developmentally at the beginning of the year as compared to the end of the year. This shows children's progress and can be understood to be attributable in part to the program's effectiveness. In programs with infants and toddlers, "analysis of assessment information may lead to changes in primary caregiver responsibilities, styles of interactions, strategies to promote language development, indoor and outdoor environments, and/or other aspects of the program" (NAEYC, 2003). In older children, assessment information gathered on developmental progress and content knowledge may lead to "changes in the daily schedule, curriculum and teaching strategies, styles of interaction, interest area arrangements, outdoor play area resources, design and implementation of activities for the whole group or for small groups" (NAEYC 2003).

Most state licensing requirements contain an annual program review that contains information about child assessment methods and results. Professional organizations set guidelines or accreditation criteria regarding the measurement of children's progress:

The NAEYC, NAECS/SDE position statement (2003) says:

Sampling is used when assessing individual children as a part of large-scale program evaluation:

- Safeguards are in place if standardized tests are used as part of evaluation

- Children's gains over time are emphasized

- Well-trained individuals conduct evaluations

- Evaluation results are publicly shared (Editor's note: This refers to program evaluation, not individual children's evaluations.)

The NAEYC Accreditation Criteria for Assessment of Child Progress Standard lists program criteria under Standard 4: Assessment of Child Progress with specific topics of:

- Creating an Assessment Plan
- Using Appropriate Methods

- Identifying Children's Interests and Needs in Describing Children's Progress

- Adapting Curriculum, Individualizing Teaching and Informing Program Development

- Communicating with Families and Involving Families in the Assessment Process

The Head Start Program Performance Standards Section 1034.21 states that:

C. (2) Staff must use a variety of strategies to promote and support

Children's learning and developmental progress based on the observations and ongoing assessment of each child

The National Association of Family Child Care Accreditation standards require observation (stated for immediate decision making), communication with families, and for reflection on practice. These all contribute to measuring children's progress as an evaluation method for program effectiveness.

1.5 The provider observes children's behavior, verbal and body language, and abilities. The provider uses this information to respond to each child. For example, the provider responds to a baby's crying as promptly and effectively as possible.

5.2 The provider is intentional and reflective in her work, thinking about what occurs with the children and their families, considering any puzzling events or concerns.

Programs are often administered by a non-profit agency with a board of directors. The program's effectiveness in meeting the mission and goals are reported to this body on a regular basis. Program assessments and aggregate totals of children's progress (not individual children) but totals such as "89% of the children in the 3- to 5-year-old classrooms rated 'on target' for language and literacy skills," or "all children were assessed using a developmental checklist as a screening tool to identify possible special needs. Five children were referred for further evaluation." Similar kinds of information may be required by private owners of early childhood facilities. Regular, systematic documentation provides the evidence that a program is using assessment for program improvement.

Programs are usually licensed by the state which may have requirements for the type and use of child and program assessments that are completed along with their frequency. Beyond licensing, programs may be evaluated and rated by outside groups or professional organizations for their compliance to criteria items set by that group. Extensive documentation of program policies and practices is gathered and submitted, then verified by the accrediting body before granting accredited status. Accreditation is a way that families can be more assured of the quality of that program. Each accrediting body has a self-study component with an assessment instrument that gathers data on how the program meets the criteria. From what you have already learned, you know that this is called a "checklist" or a "rating scale," and that it is a closed method but can be backed up by other forms of documentation. Some accreditation bodies are

(See RESOURCES for contact information)

> National Association for the Education of Young Children Program Accreditation
> National Early Childhood Program Accreditation
> National Association for Family Child Care Accreditation

DOCUMENTATION AND REPORTING OF SUSPECTED CHILD ABUSE

Unfortunately, suspected child abuse is another use for observing and documentation. Teachers, child care staff, medical personnel, and many others who work with or come in contact with children are mandated reporters, or individuals who by law must report suspicions of child abuse and maltreatment to specified agencies. The categories of abuse and maltreatment are

- Physical abuse—any non-accidental injury caused by the child's caregiver, intentional or non-intentional

- Neglect—child's physical, mental, or emotional condition has been impaired as a result of the failure to exercise a minimum degree of care such as adequate food, clothing, shelter, education, or medical attention

- Sexual abuse—includes a wide range of behavior, including exploitation thorough prostitution or pornography

- Emotional maltreatment—psychological or emotional abuse through blaming, belittling, or rejecting a child

As the teacher (or as a student), you may observe physical or behavioral indicators of abuse. Children are gaining control of their bodies so they often have bumps and bruises. Their behavior is sometimes hard to interpret, seeming strange and easily misunderstood. However, the vigilant observer takes note of injuries and behavior that is unusual. You must use your judgment; however, for the protection of the child, it is better to report suspicions than to ignore them or explain them away and later learn that the child had been suffering and no one did anything. As a student and as a professional, there are always program protocols to follow in reporting suspicions, so there are safeguards against hasty reporting. Even so, the responsibility always ultimately resides with the individual who made the observations and who suspects the child is being abused. There is no need to prove just to have reasonable cause to suspect the child is being abused. The observer is not the interrogator or the prosecutor, but is just giving authorities an alert based on factual observations.

Here are some signs to look for:

PHYSICAL ABUSE

Child's Physical Indicators	Child's Behavioral Indicators
Unexplained bruises and welts • On face, lips, mouth • On torso, back, buttocks, thighs • In various stages of healing • Clustered forming regular patterns that look like electric cord, belt buckle • On several different surface areas • Regularly appear after absence, weekend, or vacation Unexplained fractures • To skull, nose, facial structure • In various stages of healing • Multiple or spiral fractures • Swollen or tender limbs	• Wary of adult contact • Apprehensive when other children cry • Behavioral extremes: aggressiveness, withdrawal, changes in behavior • Frightened of parents • Afraid to go home • Reports injury by parents • Wears long-sleeved or similar clothing to hide injuries • Seeks affection from any adult
Unexplained burns • Cigar, cigarette burns, especially on soles, palms, back, buttocks • Immersion burns (sock-like, glove-like, doughnut-shaped on buttocks or genitalia) • Patterned like electric burner, iron, etc. • Rope burns on arms, legs, neck, or torso	
Unexplained lacerations and abrasions • To mouth, lips, gums, eyes • To external genitalia • On backs of arms, legs, or torso • Human bite marks • Frequent injuries that are "accidental" or unexplained	

MALTREATMENT/NEGLECT

Child's Physical Indicators	Child's Behavioral Indicators
• Consistent hunger, poor hygiene, inappropriate dress • Consistent lack of supervision, especially in dangerous activities or long periods • Unattended physical problems or medical or dental needs • Abandonment	• Begging or stealing food • Extended stays in school (early arrival and late departure) • Infrequent attendance at school • Constant fatigue, falling asleep in class • Alcohol and drug abuse • States there is no caretaker

EMOTIONAL MALTREATMENT

Child's Physical Indicators	Child's Behavioral Indicators
• Conduct disorders (fighting in school, anti-social, destructive, etc.) • Habit disorders (rocking, biting, sucking fingers, etc.) • Neurotic disorders (speech disorders, sleep problems, inhibition of play) • Psychoneurotic reactions (phobias, hysterical reactions, compulsion, hypochondria) • Lags in physical development • Failure to thrive	• Overly adaptive behavior (inappropriately adult or inappropriately infantile) • Developmental delays (mental, emotional) • Extremes of behavior (compliant, passive, aggressive, demanding) • Suicide attempts or gestures, self-mutilation

SEXUAL ABUSE

Child Physical Indicators	Child's Behavioral Indicators
• Difficulty in walking or sitting • Torn, stained, or bloody underclothing • Pain or itching in genital area • Pregnancy, especially in early adolescent years • Bruises or bleeding in external genital, vaginal, or anal area	• Unwilling to change for or participate in physical education classes • Withdrawal, fantasy, or infantile behavior • Bizarre, sophisticated, or unusual sexual behavior or knowledge • Self-injurious behaviors, suicide attempts • Poor peer relationships

SEXUAL ABUSE   Continued

Child Physical Indicators	Child's Behavioral Indicators
• Sexually transmitted disease (especially in pre-adolescent age group, includes venereal oral infections)	• Aggressive or disruptive behavior, delinquency, running away, or school truancy • Reports sexual assault by caretaker • Exaggerated fear of closeness or physical contact

The child may disclose to you that someone hurt them or did things to them. It is important that you not reveal your shock, revulsion, or disapproval. An appropriate response would be to gently ask, "Can you tell me what happened?" This expresses concern without probing for more details. These disclosures call for immediate action and documentation.

Documenting suspicions of child abuse or maltreatment or disclosures should be done as soon as you see or witness it. Use the old reporting technique, "who (if you know), what, when, where." The "why" you will leave to the authorities. A factual account will be needed to protect the child, get help for the family, and fulfill your obligation as a mandated reporter. Use this documentation to follow the program protocol, call the hot line in your state, and file the necessary written report. Your care in this event could save a child's life.

QUESTIONS FOR REFLECTION
More Uses of Documentation

1. It will be easy to communicate a child's progress to families, but when it comes to talking to them about the areas that are not progressing, that makes me feel _____. I wonder about _____.
I will need to _____.

2. I never thought about funders, sponsors, or administration wanting to be sure that I'm doing my job by measuring children's progress. That makes me feel _____. I can see that it is important because _____. It will make me _____
and _____.

3. I hope I never see indications of child abuse or neglect but if I do, I will _____. It makes me feel _____.
I will be sure to _____. Some other things I need to know more about are _____.

4. After learning about so many uses of documentation, I now realize _____.

CHAPTER

7

MANAGING THE PAPERWORK

All this documentation—checklists, anecdotal records, time samples, children's work, photographs, and videos—is of no use unless you have a system of filing and then finding it again.

COLLECTION SYSTEM

You will need the following:

■ File folder for each child to keep documentation separate from other children's. Pocket folders are handy for holding index cards, if you use them.

■ Child's work samples—Pizza boxes (unused of course) work well in keeping items flat.

Collecting children's work sometimes is difficult. They want to keep their products. You may be able to copy drawings and writing samples. You could take photographs of works that cannot be copied such as large paintings, sculptures, and block structures.

■ Child information form with birth date, address and important demographic data about health, family make-up, first language, and special things you should know about the child.

■ Cover sheet or index—Recordings can yield information on several developmental areas at one time. You can make notes on a cover sheet that has developmental areas on it. An anecdotal record made on 10/1 while a child looked at a book with another child may have information that tells you about the child's social development, language and literacy development, small muscle development, and attention span. A notation in each of those areas can refer back to that one record. A time sample has information on the whole class, so you would keep that in a class file, and just transfer the findings to the child's individual file in the developmental area that it documents.

- Developmental checklist.

- As a student, you will need some kind of permission or release form from the family authorizing you to observe and practice documentation. Assure the family that it is only for practice, that no confidential information will be collected, and that the child's real name will not be used in assignments. If they request it, the family has a right to a copy of any report you make on the child. Your instructor should review this first to be sure you have been tactful and accurate.

- As a practitioner, you will need an information release form signed by the child's family member before you can transfer any information about the child to an outside person or agency such as a referral agency, health professional or attorney. (This does not apply when making a child abuse report.)

- Whenever anyone other than you accesses the file, a note should be made in the file of the person's name, the date, and the reason. This contributes to the confidentiality trust between the child, the family, and the program.

PORTFOLIOS

Just as an artist assembles a collection of his or her work, you can consider the collection of documentation from your observations as a portfolio.

The portfolio contains work samples such as:

- Drawings and paintings
- Self portraits
- Child's writing

- Dictated stories

- Photographs of block building, clay sculptures, collages, even prints of dramatic play episodes captured by a digital camera

The portfolio of the child's work, supplemented by the file of the teacher's written observations, is a powerful tool in knowing the child. It is better than any test because it:

Shows progress. The child's work, behavior, and skills are seen as they develop over time. (Be sure that you date each piece of work and your observations.) The child is viewed through his or her strengths and successes rather than weaknesses.

Documents what happens naturally. The contents of the portfolio consist of the child's tasks and activities in the normal routine of the classroom, where the child is safe, comfortable, and familiar.

Focuses on the uniqueness of the child. Again, it helps to see what the child can do, not just his or her weaknesses or deficits. The child's personality is revealed through regular, accurate portrayals of work and behavior.

Informs for future planning. Looking at each child's progress helps to set goals for the next level. It recognizes successes, giving the teacher ideas about what to plan for the classroom that will build on the child's knowledge and skill and present a manageable challenge.

The child is involved in process. The children can see, add, and comment on the work samples in their portfolios, and know that you are making notes about them because what they do is important. Older children can see their progress themselves now that they are older.

Offers tangible evidence to share. Memory can be inaccurate and challenged on its authenticity, but a child's work samples and frequent, dated, non-inferential written records done over time provide irrefutable evidence. They become the centerpiece of discussions about the child.

PROTECTION OF WRITTEN RECORDS

Children's folders and portfolios need to be kept in a place where you have easy access to them. You need to be able to quickly pull out the checklists to update them and to file any notations and formal written observations. Families should know of their existence and be able to access the folder on request. Of course, no unauthorized person should have access to the folders, so here are some suggestions for their safekeeping:

- Place all folders in a portable file box.

- Keep the box in the classroom when you are there, out of children's reach but within easy reach for you.

- Be sure that all staff in the room know about the box of files and its purpose, and invite them to add their written observations as well.

- Place the box in a locked cabinet in the classroom or remove it to an office that is kept locked in off-hours.

- When families want to see their own child's file, be sure that they see only that file. You can do this by personally removing the file and handing it to them.

- As a student, be sure to check with the classroom teacher before giving any documents to the family.

At the end of the school year, or when the child moves into the next classroom or leaves the program, there should be a policy about what happens to the file. It may be passed on to the next teacher or sent with the family to the next program. It may be given to the family to keep for their records or it may be kept by the program. Teachers must be sure that there is nothing in the file other than records that pertain or refer to that particular child.

QUESTIONS FOR REFLECTION
Managing the Paperwork

1. It seems like this is much more than I ever thought I'd be doing as a teacher. It makes me _____. I've learned that in order to do it I'll need to _____.

2. In thinking about managing the paperwork, I have special skills in _____ _____. That will help me to _____. An area I will especially need to work on is _____. I can seek help from _____.

3. In gathering documentation on each child into a portfolio, I see that _____ _____. An idea I have about it is _____. I wonder if _____. I think the child will feel _____.

4. To protect my documentation as a student, I must remember to _____ _____. When I am in the classroom, I will _____. When I am the teacher I think that I will need to _____.

CHAPTER

8

ETHICS AND CONFIDENTIALITY

As professionals, we are held to a higher standard to do the right thing and to maintain the client's privileged information. This is true for several reasons.

FAIRNESS

We are only human, with likes, dislikes, and biases that have been established from our own childhood, upbringing, the media, and the culture in which we were raised. When we observe and assess children, those factors should not enter into our documentation. By selecting objective methods that just record the facts, or using checklists that draw on objective, predetermined criteria against which to measure, we strive to collect and record data about a child that is honest. This means that we do *not:*

- Write about an incident long after it has occurred. Our memories may not be accurate after time has passed.

- Make inferences about a child based on one isolated incident.

- Take an event out of context to draw conclusions about the child.

- Place the child outside of the normal environment or routine and expect to obtain factual information about the child's knowledge or development.

- Label the whole child based on single factors (cute, smart, bad/good, hyperactive/passive, naughty, vicious, cruel, bullying).

- Only select observations to write about that portray the child in a negative (or positive) light, but select randomly or typical behavior to record.

- Write often about some children and seldom about others.

The purpose of using various recording methods with children and observing at different times of day in a systematic way is to randomize the observations, eliminating some of the possibility of unfair portrayals. If the observations are highly selective, such as only writing anecdotal records about misbehavior or extraordinary events, the documentation on the child is slanted and unfair. When end-of-the-day, diary-type notations, are made, memories are often of just misbehavior or extraordinary events, and miss the routine, normal behavior that probably makes up most of the day and most of the children's activities. That leaves little to remember about those children who follow the rules and are quiet. However, you could write pages about other children. A systematic plan for the observation of each child, using multiple methods, results in a fairer assessment of development and record of behavior and interactions.

ASSESSMENT AND CULTURE

Almost one-third of the U.S. population is non-white. Almost half of the U.S. population learns another language than English as their first language. Half of the immigrant families in the United States live below the federal poverty line, read to their children less often, are less likely to take their children on outings or to volunteer at school or community functions. Immigrant children are four times as likely to be in fair or poor health compared to children born in the United States. Race, age, gender, country of origin, home language, lifestyles, and family belief systems all contribute to cultural diversity, impacting:

- Beliefs and values

- Behavioral expectations

- Family and social roles

- Spiritual beliefs and practices

- Economic systems

- Language

- Customs and practices

- Attainment of developmental milestones

Possible consequences of assessment that does not give consideration to the child's culture could result in an over-referral rate, diagnosis or labeling of "special needs," and inappropriate intervention. In assessment outside of the cultural context:

- Behaviors might be misinterpreted

- Competence in other languages may be mistaken for a language delay in English.

- Devaluing cultures or language may lower self-esteem and self-confidence

- Divergent sets of expectations between home and school place the child in a compromising position of choosing one over the other

- Real disabilities or delays may be overlooked when attributed to language or culture

The observer must use extra care to describe behavior without making judgments, inferences, or decisions, taking into consideration the cultural context.

In recognition of the dramatic rise in ethnic diversity in the United States, the National Association for the Education of Young Children has added a supplement to the position statement on curriculum, assessment, and program evaluation. It has adopted a position statement on Screening and Assessment of Young English-Language Learners (NAEYC 2005). The recommendations are:

(1) Adaptations should be made to assessments of a child whose home language is not English to determine what further supports and services are needed. The assessments are used primarily to understand and improve children's learning. When assessments are made for program evaluation and accountability, adaptations assure that all children's assessments are included but that they do not negatively impact the results.

(2) Assessment tools and procedures should align with cultural and linguistic characteristics of the child. Assessments are made in the home language, and are reviewed for cultural appropriateness by native speakers of that home language.

(3) Assessments help the program support learning and development of young English-language learners by relying on systematic, multiple, age-appropriate observational assessment methods, repeated over time by more than one person.

(4) Where appropriate standardized formal assessments are used, decision makers accommodate for young English-language learners' needs to be included but fairly assessed.

(5) Assessments are made by those with cultural and linguistic competence, child development knowledge, and assessment knowledge and skills. They are known to the child and familiar with second language acquisition.

(6) Families are involved in the assessment selection and implementation, and informed of results.

(7) The field should attend to the development of better assessment measures for young English language learners, and policy makers and higher education institutions should work to recruit and retain a diverse early childhood workforce to support young English language learners.

CONFIDENTIALITY

We talk about what happens in our everyday lives, about things that interest or concern us, and about the actions of others. Human nature leads us to talk about children's behavior, events in the classroom, or about the child's family. We are tempted to talk about the children with friends and our own families. When we do this, we can be breaching the confidentiality of "client-privileged information." What a patient tells a doctor or a client tells an attorney is not divulged. It is supposed to be kept private between them. When we observe children and write down what they do and say, we come to know them so well. And what we write down we remember (that's why we make lists). We must limit our tendency to talk about the children because of our dedication to professionalism. We must never use children's real names when we use them as illustrations. We must never tell stories about children that could be embarrassing if the family heard it. We must never make critical remarks to others about how another teacher is dealing with a child. If the behavior may be harmful, it will be communicated to the supervisor.

The NAEYC (2005) Code of Ethics says:

Principle 2.8—We shall treat child assessment information confidentially and share this information only when there is a legitimate need for it.

Principle 2.13—We shall maintain confidentiality and shall respect the family's right to privacy, refraining from disclosure of confidential information and intrusion into family life.

As a student, you protect the children's identity by changing their names or just using initials in written work. You do not divulge derogatory information or stories about the teacher or the program to other students in class. If you have concerns about what you see, you can ask the teacher of the classroom to explain. Perhaps in your limited view or time there, you are misinterpreting or misunderstanding what is going on. If you are not comfortable asking this type of question there, or if you feel you have a firm understanding but just do not agree with policy or procedure, philosophy, or practice, then you can write about this in your journal and discuss it privately with your instructor. Of course, if you see a child in danger or staff members performing dangerous or illegal actions, it is your responsibility to report that to the appropriate person immediately.

When you are the teacher, the same ethical behavior of protecting the rights of the child and the privacy of the family hold true. Notes and written observations should be kept concealed during and after you use them and filed in a place that is not accessible to people not authorized to view them. Discussions with coworkers about a child or a family are important ways to verify your own inferences and judgments, but they must be kept professional, eliminating hearsay, gossip, and derogatory or accusatory statements. Outside of the program, among other professionals, you will of course discuss your own experiences. This is a way of gaining outside perspective on events and children's behavior and broadening your own viewpoint. This can and should be done without identifying the child or family. Again, your aim is to gain perspective, not to ridicule or cause outrage. With family and friends, you portray people, events, and situations without any identification and solely for discussion or illustration, not mockery or derision.

Probably no other area of our professional practice is more at risk than our ethical behavior. In dealing with people, we can never anticipate what strange circumstances will occur. It is not always clear what is the "right" action to take. Our own background and emotions can sometimes overshadow our knowledge and good judgment. Remember that phrase that we use with children, "How would you like it if she did that to you?"

QUESTIONS FOR REFLECTION
Ethics and Confidentiality

1. I will try to be fair in my observations by _____.
   I think this will help me because _____. An
   area that I will have to be careful of is _____. I'll do this
   by _____.

2. I was raised with the ideas that children should _____
   _____. When children don't, it
   makes me _____. In my work I will
   have to _____.

3. A culture that I need to know more about is _____
   _____. I can try to find out by _____
   _____. This will be important because _____.
   I really want to _____.

4. It seems to me that the hardest part about confidentiality is _____
   _____. I never thought about
   _____. I will need to remember _____
   _____. I have heard _____.
   I think that person should _____. The next time I
   hear something like that I will _____. I will have to
   watch myself that _____.

PROFESSIONAL ORGANIZATIONS

National Association for the Education of Young Children (NAEYC)
1313 L. Street, N.W., Suite 500
Washington, DC 20005
800-424-2460
Web site: www.naeyc.org
E-mail: membership@naeyc.org

Specific membership benefits:

Comprehensive members receive all the benefits of regular membership described below, plus annually receive five or six books immediately after their release by NAEYC.

Regular and student members receive:

- Six issues of *Young Children*, which includes timely articles on pertinent issues, as well as suggestions and strategies for enhancing children's learning
- Reduced registration fees at NAEYC-sponsored local and national conferences and seminars
- Discounted prices on hundreds of books, videos, brochures, and posters from NAEYC's extensive catalog of materials
- Access to the members only Web site, including links to additional resources and chat sites for communication with other professionals

National Association of Child Care Professionals (NACCP)
P.O. Box 90723
Austin, TX 78709
800-537-1118
Web site: www.naccp.org

Specific membership benefits:

Management Tools of the Trade™ Your membership provides complete and free access (a $79 value) to effective management tools that provide technical assistance in human resource management. In addition, members will receive NACCP's quarterly trade journals, *Professional Connections©, Teamwork©,* and *Caring for Your Children©, to help you stay* on top of hot issues in child care. Each edition also includes a *Tool of the Trade™.*

National Child Care Association (NCCA)
1016 Rosser Street
Conyers, GA 30012
800-543-7161
Web site: www.nccanet.org

Specific membership benefits:

- As the only recognized voice in Washington DC, NCCA has great influence on legislators

- Professional development opportunities

Association for Childhood Education International (ACEI)
The Olney Professional Building
17904 Georgia Avenue, Suite 215
Olney, MD 20832
Phone: 800-423-2563 or 301-570-2122
Fax: 301-570-2212
Web site: www.acei.org
ACEI is an international organization dedicated to promoting the best educational practices throughout the world.

Specific membership benefits:

- Workshops and travel/study tours abroad

- Four issues per year of the journals Childhood Education and Journal of Research in Childhood Education

- Hundreds of resources for parents and teachers, including books, pamphlets, audiotapes, and videotapes

National AfterSchool Association (NAA)
1137 Washington Street
Boston, MA 02124
Phone: 617-298-5012
Fax: 617-298-5022
Web site: www.naaweb.org

NAA is a national organization dedicated to providing information, technical assistance, and resources concerning children in out-of-school programs. Members include teachers, policy makers, and administrators representing all public, private, and community-based sectors of after-school programs.

Specific member benefits:

- A subscription to the NAA journal, *School-Age Review*
- A companion membership in state affiliates
- Discounts on NAA publications and products
- Discount on NAA annual conference registration
- Opportunity to be an NAA accreditation endorser
- Public policy representatives in Washington, DC

OTHER ORGANIZATIONS TO CONTACT:

The Children's Defense Fund
25 E. Street, N.W.
Washington DC, 20001
202-628-8787
Web site: www.childrensdefense.org

National Association for Family Child Care
P.O. Box 10373
Des Moines, IA 50306
800-359-3817
Web site: www.nafcc.org
Journal: The National Perspective

National Black Child Development Institute
1023 15th Avenue, N.W.
Washington, DC 20002
202-833-2220
Web site: www.nbcdi.org

National Head Start Association
1651 Prince Street
Alexandria, VA 22314
703-739-0875
Web site: www.nhsa.org
Journal: Children and Families

International Society for the Prevention of Child Abuse and Neglect
25 W. 560 Geneva Road, Suite L2C
Carol Stream, IL 60188
630-221-1311

Web site: www.ispcan.org
Journal: *Child Abuse and Neglect: The International Journal*

Council for Exceptional Children
1110 N. Glebe Road, Suite 300
Arlington, VA 22201
888-CEC-SPED
Web site: www.cec.sped.org
Journal: *CEC Today*

National Association for Bilingual Education
Union Center Plaza
810 First Street, N.E.
Washington, DC 20002
Web site: www.nabe.org
Journal: NABE Journal of Research and Practice

International Reading Association
800 Barksdale Road
P.O. Box 8139
Newark, DE 19714
800-336-READ
Web site: www.reading.org
Journal: The Reading Teacher

National Education Organization (NEA)
1201 16th Street, N.W.
Washington, DC 20036
202-833-4000
Web site: www.nea.org
Journals: *Works4Me* and *NEA Focus* (by online subscription)

Zero to Three: National Center for Infants, Toddlers, and Families
2000 M. Street, N.W., Suite 200
Washington, DC 20036
202-638-1144
Web site: www.zerotothree.org
Journal: Zero to Three

RESOURCES ON OBSERVATION AND ASSESSMENT

BOOKS

Allen, K. E., & Marotz, L. R. (2007). *Developmental profiles: Pre-birth through twelve,* 5th ed. Clifton Park, NY: Thomson Delmar Learning.

Almy, M., & Genishi, C. (1979). *Ways of studying children.* New York: Teachers College Press.

Aloha, D., & Kovacik, A. (2007). *Observing and understanding child development: A child study manual.* Clifton Park, NY: Thomson Delmar Learning.

Beaty, J. (2006). *Observing development of the young child,* 6th ed. New York: Pearson Merrill Prentice Hall.

Benner, S. M. (2003). *Assessment of young children with special needs: A context-approach.* Clifton Park, NY: Thomson Delmar Learning.

Bentzen, W. R., & Frost, M. B. (2003). *Seeing child care: A guide for assessing the effectiveness of child care programs.* Clifton Park, NY: Thomson Delmar Learning.

Bentzen, W. R. (2005). *Seeing young children: A guide to observing and recording behavior,* 5th ed. Clifton Park, NY: Thomson Delmar Learning.

Cohen, D., Stern, V., & Balaban, N. (1997). *Observing and recording the behavior of young children,* 4th ed. New York: Teachers College Press.

Colker, L. J. (1995). *Observing young children: Learning to look, looking to learn.* Washington, DC: Teaching Strategies.

Curtis, D., & Carter, M. (2006). *The art of awareness: How observation can transform your teaching.* New York: Thomson Prentice Hall.

Dichtelmiller, M., Jablon, J. R., Dorfman, A B., Mardsden, D. B., & Meisels, S. J. (1997). *Work sampling in the classroom: A teacher's manual.* Ann Arbor, MI: Rebus, Inc.

Ensher, G. L., Bobish, T. P., Gardner, E. F., Reinson, C. L., Bryden, D. A., & Foertsch, D. J. (2007). *Partners in play: Assessing infants and toddlers in natural contexts.* Clifton Park, NY: Thomson Delmar Learning.

Gober, S. Y. (2002). *Six simple ways to assess young children.* Clifton Park, NY: Thomson Delmar Learning.

Harms, T., Clifford, R. M., & Cryer, D. (2005). *Early childhood environment rating scale, revised edition.* New York: Teachers College Press.

Helm, J. H., Beneke, S., & Steinheimer, K. (1998). *Windows on learning: Documenting young children's work.* New York: Teachers College Press.

Jablon, J. R., Dombro, A. L., & Dichtelmiller, M. L. (1999). *The power of observation.* Washington, DC: Teaching Strategies.

Leonard, A. M. (1997). *I spy something: A practical guide to classroom observation of young children.* Little Rock: Southern Early Childhood Association.

MacDonald, S. (2005). *The portfolio and its use: A road map for assessment,* 2nd ed. Little Rock: Southern Early Childhood Association.

McAfee, O., & Leong, D. (2007). *Assessing and guiding young children's development and learning,* 4th ed. Boston: Pearson Allyn & Bacon.

Meisels, S. J., & Atkins-Burnett, S. (2005). *Developmental screening in early childhood: A guide,* 5th ed. Washington, DC: National Association for the Education of Young Children.

Mindes, G. (2007). *Assessing young children.* New York: Thomson Prentice Hall.

(2005). *NAEYC early childhood program standards and accreditation criteria.* National Association for the Education of Young Children. Washington, DC.

Nilsen, B. A. (2008). *Week by week: Documenting the development of young children,* 4th ed. Clifton Park, NY: Thomson Delmar Learning.

Shores, E. F., & Grace, C. (2005). *The portfolio book.* New York: Thomson Prentice Hall.

INTERNET RESOURCES

www.aasa.org
The Web site of the American Association of School Administrators provides access to past and current issues of *The School Administrator,* a journal providing articles on best practices for beginning readers.

www.acf.dhhs.gov
U.S. Department of Health and Human Services, Office of Children and Families includes information on how to report child abuse, initiatives, and laws.

www.allianceforchildhood.net
The Alliance for Childhood is committed to fostering and respecting each child's inherent right to a healthy, developmentally appropriate childhood. The site includes information on toys, computers, and play in regard to how it affects learning.

www.apa.org
The American Psychological Association offers information on ethics, continuing education, and codes of conduct.

www.asha.org
The American Speech-Language-Hearing Association provides information on all areas of speech, language, and hearing, including bilingual.

www.autism-society.org
The Autism Society of America site offers vast information regarding spectrum disorders.

www.babylab.rutgers.edu
This Web site is the home of the Infancy Studies Laboratory at Rutgers University.

www.bankstreet.edu
Bank Street College, a leader in child-centered education, provides information regarding early childhood literacy development, available programs, and professional development.

www.cal.org
The Center for Applied Linguistics Web site provides a wide range of information including research, teacher education, design and development of instructional materials, technical assistance, conference planning, program evaluation, and policy analysis.

www.cdipage.com
This comprehensive child development site by the Child Development Institute includes information on the stages of development as described by Piaget.

www.chadd.org
The Web site of Children and Adults with Attention-Deficit/ Hyperactivity Disorder (CHADD) offers information on the disorder, including the first online library for ADHD.

www.childdevelopmentinfo.com
The Child Development & Parenting Information Web site provides information on child development, learning, health and safety. This site also provides resources and suggestions for parents of toddlers to teens.

www.childtrendsdatabank.org
The Child Trends Databank provides the latest national trends and research on over 80 key indicators of child and youth well-being.

www.csee.net
The Center for Social and Emotional Education provides resources, services, consults, and projects to support educators and parents.

www.earlychildhood.com
Earlychildhood.com provides resources for lessons, conferences, products, etc.

www.ecrp.uiuc.edu
Early Childhood Research & Practice is an Internet journal dedicated to the development, care, and education of young children. The site includes information on the philosophy and art of the Reggio Emilia approach to preschool education, which uses technology as a tool of the mind, and other topics.

www.ed.gov
The U.S. Department of Education Web site provides information on the No Child Left Behind Act, which was passed in an effort to facilitate educational reform.

www.emc.cmich.edu
The Educational Materials Center contains the standards and benchmarks for health and physical education from Central Michigan University.

www.emtech.net
emTech has extensive links to many sites about brain development.

www.enfamil.com

The Enfamil (makers of baby formula) Web site provides a description of physical development and activities from birth to 5 years old.

www.eric.ed.gov

Use this database of the Education Resources Information Center to search for educational literature. The site includes information regarding portfolios and their use.

www.extension.iastate.edu

Iowa State University publications cover topics including child abuse and child development.

www.fairtest.org

The National Center for Fair & Open Testing is an advocacy organization working to end the abuses, misuses, and flaws of standardized testing and ensure that evaluation of students and workers is fair, open, and educationally sound.

www.famlit.org

The National Center for Family Literacy encourages families to read to and with their children.

www.fen.com

The Family Education Network provides vast resources for families.

www.fpg.unc.edu

The Frank Porter Graham Child Development Institute Web site provides information regarding the study of young children and their families.

www.halls.md

This Web site provides health calculators and charts.

www.healthychildcare.org

The American Academy of Pediatrics provides information on health and safety standards for home and child care.

www.highscope.org

This Web site provides information about the High/Scope program and its products and assessments.

www.icaf.org

The International Child Art Foundation enhances children's creative potential and fosters global harmony.

www.isbe.state.il.us
The Web site of the Illinois State Board of Education offers state school standards for physical development and health.

www.katsnet.org
The Kentucky Assistive Technology Service (KATS) Network Co-ordinating Center Web site provides information on assistive technology and the IEP.

www.kidsafe-caps.org
The Child Abuse Prevention Services (CAPS) includes a listing of state-by-state child abuse reporting hotline numbers, information on how to report child abuse, resources, and links.

www.kidshealth.org
The KidsHealth Web site is presented by the Nemours Foundation, and provides information on child health and development.

www.macbrain.org
The Research Network on Early Experience and Brain Development explores how knowledge of brain development can guide us in our understanding of behavioral development and vice versa.

www.mea-mft.org
This is a Web-based guidebook for new teachers, specifically in Montana. Information can be applied elsewhere and is geared toward providing important information and tools for new educators.

www.nacd.org
The National Association for Child Development Web site offers a wide range of information on talented and gifted and learning disorders.

www.naeyc.org
The National Association for the Education of Young Children Web site provides information, resources, and position statements on a variety of educational topics.

www.nafcc.org
The National Association for Family Child Care Web site provides information on conferences, accreditation, and membership.

www.nameorg.org
The National Association of Multicultural Education provides information regarding diversity and multicultural education.

www.childwelfare.gov
The Child Welfare Information Gateway provides access to information and resources to help protect children and strengthen families.

www.nccic.org
The National Child Care Information Center Web site provides articles on brain development for parents and caregivers.

www.ncrel.org
The North Central Regional Educational Laboratory (NCREL) Web site provides high-quality, research-based resources to educators. The pathways to school improvement section provides information to those engaged in school improvement and those looking for information on how to improve their teaching skills.

www.necpa.net
The National Early Childhood Program Accreditation Web site provides information on how NECPA works, how to enroll, and mentoring.

www.netc.org
The Northwest Educational Technology Consortium offers resources and information for educators and care providers regarding technology in early childhood education and how to connect technology with the way young children learn.

www.nidcd.nih.gov
The National Institute on Deafness and Other Communication Disorders offers information related to hearing, balance, smell, taste, voice, speech, and language.

www.ninds.nih.gov
The National Institute of Neurological Disorders and Stroke provides an index of many kinds of neurological disorders.

www.nncc.org
The National Network for Child Care Web site provides educational articles and resources on a variety of topics, and lists child care-related conferences and events.

www.nsastutter.org
The National Stuttering Association offers information about helping preschoolers, school-age children, and teenagers who stutter.

www.ohioline.osu.edu
The Ohio State University offers access to hundreds of fact sheets, bulletins, and other educational materials covering agriculture, natural resources, family and consumer sciences, community development, 4H, and youth.

www.parentcenter.com
The ParentCenter Web site provides information and resources for parents and educators regarding developmental milestones (ages 2–8).

www.patnc.org
The Parents as Teachers Web site provides resources on programs designed to enhance child development through parent education.

www.pbs.org
The Public Broadcasting System Web site provides resources for teachers regarding lesson plans, physical development, and how to use television for learning.

www.pta.org
The National Parent Teacher Association Web site provides information on conferences and resources.

www.rif.org
Reading Is Fundamental is the nation's largest children's literacy organization. Its Web site has information for educators, including book lists and promotions.

www.spacesforchildren.net
Network Solutions features photographs and layouts of spaces for children that help child care facilities create developmentally appropriate environments.

www.successforall.net
The Success for All Foundation uses research to design programs and services that help schools better meet the needs of all their students.

www.teachers.net
Teachers.Net is a resource for educators featuring the "Gazette," a publication with teaching tips, lessons, and classroom activities.

www.uni.edu
Visit The National Program for Playground Safety Information Web site and test your knowledge of playground safety!

www.vanderbilt.edu
This site provides access to projects that focus on promoting social/emotional education in young children.

www.zerotothree.org
The Zero to Three Web site supports the healthy development and well-being of infants, toddlers, and their families.

www2.edc.org
The National Center to Improve Practice in Special Education Through Technology, Media, and Materials offers a collection of resources.

CONTENT STANDARDS SET BY PROFESSIONAL ORGANIZATIONS

Art—*National Visual Arts Standards*—National Art Education Association www.naea.org

English—*Standards for the English Language Arts*—National Council of Teachers of English and International Reading Association www.ncte.org

English as a Second Language—*ESL Standards for Pre-K–12 Students*—Teachers of English to Speakers of Other Languages www.tesol.org

Head Start—*Head Start Child Outcomes Framework*—Department of Health and Human Services www.headstartinfo.org

Health Education—*National Health Education Standards*—American Association for Health Education www.aahperd.org

High/scope®—*Key Experiences*—High/Scope www.highscope.org

Mathematics—*Principles and Standards for School Mathematics*—National Council of Teachers of Mathematics www.nctm.org

Music—*Benchmarks in Action: Standards-Based Assessment in Music*—The National Association for Music Education www.menc.org

Science—*Benchmarks for Science Literacy*—American Association for the Advancement of Science www.project2061.org

Social Studies—*Expectations of Excellence*—National Council on Social Studies www.ncss.org

Technology—*National Educational Technology Standards*—International Society for Technology in Education www.cnets.iste.org

B

CASE STUDIES

Here are some situations that you may face as a student while observing in classrooms. Write down what you would do or say.

WHAT WOULD YOU DO OR SAY?

1. You are a student doing observations in a classroom of 4 year olds for an assignment. You are busily drawing a diagram of the classroom and making notes about which children are playing in the various areas. A child comes over and asks, "What are you doing?"

   What would you say/do?

   _____

   _____

   You could say:

   > "I'm learning about being a teacher and I'm drawing your classroom so I can remember how it is set up. See, here is the easel and art area, here is the water table, here is the table and chairs where you eat. You'd better return to your work and I'll do my work here. Where are you going to play next?"

   > If you are a practitioner and the child asks you this question, your answer would be the same.

2. You are a student doing observations in a classroom of 4 year olds for an assignment. You are busily drawing a diagram of the classroom and making notes about which children are playing in the various areas. A child comes over and asks, "Can I write too?" and, before you realize

what is happening, the child has grabbed your pen and is writing all over your assignment!

What would you say?

_____

_____

You could say:

"I'll find you a paper and pencil so you can write like I am. I'm drawing a map of the classroom. Want to try it?"

If you are a practitioner and the child asks you this question, your answer would be the same.

3. You are a student doing observations in a classroom of toddlers. You see a child climbing up on a bookcase out of the view of the teacher, who is talking to a parent at the door. Another teacher is attending to a crying child.

What would you say or do?

_____

_____

You could say/do:

Of course, the safety of a child is more important than any written work. If neither teacher is available or does not see the situation, you should take action and help the child down.

If you are a practitioner in this situation, the answer would be the same. Drop the writing and give attention to the child's safety.

4. You are a student or practitioner filling in a child development checklist on a particular child. It is fascinating. You have been watching the child, filling in the various areas of development that you see. The child looks up and sees you watching. The child stops what she is doing, moves to another area, looks up, and sees that you are still watching. The child then crouches down behind a chair and peeks out at you with a serious look on her face.

What would you say or do?

_____

_____

You could say/do:

Go over to the child, get down on her level, and say gently, "I know that you have seen me watching you. I'm writing down on this paper all the things that you can do. I saw that you can climb the ladder and slide down the slide, that you can use the glue and scissors all by yourself, and that you really like to look at books. I'm learning about all the things you can do. Now I'll watch some other child and see what she can do." Stop watching this child for a while or for the day because it is obvious that you are making her uncomfortable. If you are a student, you may want to write a note of explanation on your uncompleted assignment.

5. You are a student observing and documenting a particular child in the classroom with a running record, writing down everything the child does and says over a 15-minute period. Whew! That was hard because this child was all over the place—a living tornado. She tipped over chairs, threw books, knocked other children's coats off the cubbie hooks. She splashed paint on someone else's paper, and repeatedly ignored the teacher's attempts to direct her activities and prevent further mayhem. It is obvious that this child is hyperactive or else the teacher is incompetent.

What would you say?

_____

_____

You could say/do:

First of all, it is good that you have documentation about this child's behavior. It may indeed be true that this child has some kind of a problem or behavior disorder. However, diagnosing the child as hyperactive based on a 15-minute observation is both professionally and medically unethical. And inferring that the teacher is ineffective is also unethical. So what can you do? At the conclusion of your session there you could say, "My observation today was of XX and is full of details about a busy 15 minutes. Would you like a copy of my observation? Is there anything that you are allowed to tell me about her behavior today so that I can better understand it?"

If you are a practitioner noting this kind of behavior in a child you will want more than this one day's observing and documenting. Then you may want to discuss this with the child's family, using your documentation. You should also examine the classroom environment and the curriculum to see if these may be contributing factors to the child's behavior. You would try to intervene and find something of interest for the child to do, harnessing the energy in constructive pursuits.

6. A parent sees you writing down observations of his child in the classroom and confronts you with, "Who are you, and what are you doing watching my child and taking notes? I want a copy of everything you've written about my child."

What would you say?

_____

_____

You could say/do:

(Smile, hold out your hand to shake and introduce yourself.) "Hello, I'm XX from YY college, where I'm a student in child development. I believe that a letter went home informing the families about my role here, and was signed by a family member. I'm learning about child development by using various observation methods. All the information is confidential and all children's names are masked in my assignments. You can check with the teacher, but I'm sure that every child in this class has a signed permission form for me to do this. Perhaps it was another family member who signed the form. There was a spot on the form to check if the family wanted a copy of any observations. We can look at the form and see if that was checked and if not, we can do that. You'll receive that after my assignments have been graded by my professor. It will come back to you through the teacher. I know it can be disconcerting to see someone watching your child. This is a very active, interesting class, and I'm learning a lot from observing all the children."

If you are the practitioner in this situation, you could refer to the parent handbook and parent orientation where you explained your gathering of developmental information through observation and documentation, and that the notes on their own child are always open for parents to read.

7. You are visiting a classroom, doing observation assignments, and the teacher says, "Oh, it's nice you are learning to do that, but you'll never use that in a real classroom because you'll be too busy."

What would you say?

_____

_____

You could say:

"I know the teacher's role is a really busy one. I've watched you and I don't know how you keep track of all you have to do. But in our class, we are learning about setting up an observation schedule so that regularly scheduled observations on each child should be more manageable. I'd be willing to bring you a copy and you could look it over."

If you are the practitioner and you are too busy to take notes, then you will want to examine your classroom environment, curriculum, and routines to see if they are too teacher directed. You should always have pen and paper handy to jot down short notes to amplify later when there is more time. You may try to get some help in the classroom to allow you some observation time.

8. You are out with your friends and you say, "In the classroom where I was observing, Jeremy Watkins went over behind the chair, pulled down his pants, and pooped right there on the floor! Yuck! I wonder how the teacher could stand to clean it up, and I wonder if he does that at home. His mother is one of these uppity types. I overheard the director talking with her about her unpaid tuition bill. Wouldn't you know!"

One of the people in your group says, "Jeremy Watkins, who lives on Maplewood? His mother is my cousin!"

What about this?

You should say:

"Oh, no! I can't believe what I just said! Even if no one here knew the child or family, those were unprofessional and unkind things to say. I am so sorry that I said it. I wasn't thinking and just blurted it out. Please don't repeat what I said. My own biases are really the problem here. I hope I've learned my lesson about confidentiality."

There are several grievous slips here: Talking about a child by name, relating an incident for the entertainment of others, speaking disrespectfully of a child's parent, and repeating overheard information. Of course, what is said cannot be taken back. Admission of the breach of confidentiality and request to disregard it is the first step. There may be later ramifications if the story is related to others, especially to the family. Be prepared to take responsibility for the error and make appropriate apologies. You should also consider talking to the director about the incident so that he or she is prepared if there is fallout from the family. Let this incident remain as a warning—so YOU are not caught in such a situation—by making it a rule to refrain from speaking about children, their actions, and their families to people who should not hear about it. On the other hand, the professional reasons for relating observed incidents would be to share observations, ask questions for deeper understanding, and receive advice from colleagues. As we do that, we would first remove our personal feelings, personal biases, and overheard comments, then seek to better understand how to meet the needs of the child.

You are the practitioner whose professionalism has slipped and you have made this terrible statement. It is even more serious for you must face that child and family every day. Some reflection is in order, examining realistic child expectations, and biases about children and families. A personal reflection log may give you an outlet to express your feelings and help to work through them for a healthier, more professional attitude.

WRITING NOTES TO THE FAMILY

The teacher asks you to write notes to the families of the five children that you observed this week, updating them on what you have seen in their development. This is what you have written about each child. Now you are the instructor. How would you rate these responses? What revisions would you suggest to the student to bring them in line with what you have learned?

EXERCISE: UNDERLINE ANY QUESTIONABLE PASSAGES AND GIVE SUGGESTIONS FOR REVISION

CHILD 1: "I've enjoyed observing Clarissa this week. Thanks for the opportunity. I reviewed the area of social development and noted that she has many different play-mates in the classroom, playing mostly in the dramatic play area with them. She loves the dress-up clothes and I saw her lead three other children in a 10-minute-long episode about preparing a meal for company. She used words like menu, nutritious. She took turns, and only sought out the teacher when she couldn't remove the top from one of the containers. She led the other children in cleanup."

What revisions would you make?

_____

_____

Child 1: *This needs no revisions. It is friendly in tone and descriptive.*

CHILD 2: "I observed Dominick this week as a part of my coursework at the college. Thank you for the opportunity. I saw that he is still adjusting to the classroom since I understand he just was transferred into this class 2 weeks ago. He hasn't yet made a friend, playing alone most of the time, spending a great deal of time in the block area. I saw him build an intricate building and am attaching a photograph of it. No other children in the class build like this."

What revisions would you suggest?

_____

_____

Child 2: *He hasn't yet made a friend, playing alone most of the time, spending... He spends a great deal of time in the block area. I saw him build an intricate building and am attaching a photograph of it. No other children in the class build like this.*

It is not unusual for a child to spend time alone. The comment about not making friends might be alarming to the family and judgmental on the part of the observer.

CHILD 3: "I observed Luciana this week as a part of my coursework at the college. Since I do not speak her language, I couldn't tell what she was saying, but I saw her leading the teacher by the hand to show what she wanted, making her needs clearly known. She wouldn't say any words out loud but did whisper some to another child in the class. Perhaps if you would teach her some phrases like "May I have that, please?" and "Want to play?" it would help her develop English and play skills."

What revisions would you suggest?

_____

_____

Child 3: Perhaps if you would teach her some phrases like "May I have that, please?" and "Want to play?" it would help her develop English and play skills. *I understand the school is providing an interpreter for all notes, including this one, and for when you come to school. Perhaps you could teach us all some common words and phrases so we can communicate with her and you.*

We should not give advice to the family like this. Hopefully the school will be able to accommodate the home language.

CHILD 4: "I had a great time in Ms Crimmins' class this week, getting to know the children, and exercising my observing skills for my college coursework. I especially liked observing Daryl and Darius. Observing twins and seeing how they are alike and different was a great experience for me. I learned from my observation that Daryl is the leader and Darius is the follower. Daryl likes rough and tumble play and Darius is more cautious and hangs back, afraid to get hurt. I didn't see them play with other children much. They are a bit smaller than the rest of the children in the class but maybe that's because they are twins."

What revisions would you suggest?

_____

_____

Child 4: I learned from my observation that Daryl is the leader and Darius is the follower. Daryl likes rough and tumble play and Darius is more cautious and hangs back, afraid to get hurt. I didn't see them play with other children much. They are a bit smaller than the rest of the children in the class but maybe that's because they are twins.

Daryl likes large muscle, active play and Darius prefers creative activities such as painting and block building. They often play with each other during the day.

The comparison is only natural, but the observation comments should be descriptive and not inferential. We do not know what "a bit smaller" means, but is not the role of the student observer to make comments about that area of development. The wondering is a part of your diary or journal entry, not for a note home.

CHILD 5: "I'm a student in a child development class who has been observing in Marika's class this week. I focused all my observations on her. Because she is so much smaller than the rest of the children, she looks like a toddler compared to the other 4 year olds. When I did the checklist, I saw that she really did only reach the late toddler stage in most areas. I would recommend that you have her evaluated right away for developmental delays and for placement in the city's program for special needs children."

What revisions would you suggest?

_____

_____

Child 5: "Because she is so much smaller than the rest of the children, she looks like a toddler compared to the other 4 year olds. When I did the checklist, I saw that she really did only reach the late toddler stage in most areas. I would recommend that you have her evaluated right away for developmental delays and for placement in the city's program for special needs children."

I am practicing my observation and recording skills using different methods and today I made the following notes about Marika. As Marika proceeded through the day's activities, she was able to place pegs in a pegboard and follow simple directions. She also recognized herself in class pictures. Thank you for the opportunity to observe Marika.

It is not the role of the student observer to divulge developmental information, especially if it is about red flags, to anyone other than the teacher of the classroom. It may be helpful for the teacher if you share your checklist, observations, and concerns with him or her.

CHILD 6: I obsered your child Stepanie for 3 weeks this semster and lerned a lot. She can walk, talk, play like other chilren even tho she is handicapt. I tink she will do fine in kindegarden.

What revisions would you suggest?

_____

_____

Child 6: Perhaps you noticed several misspelled words in this note, maybe even the child's name! Some people have difficulty with spelling and, if you are one of them, then everything that you write as a student and as a teacher should be spell-checked. Computers are wonderful at that, but sometimes you will need to handwrite a note. Be sure to have someone else look it over. There is no shame in that, but there is a bigger problem if you send home a note from the "teacher" that contains spelling errors.

Another problem area with this note is that it is not specific regarding what the child can do, and refers in a demeaning way to the child's disability. The note could read:

I have observed Stephanie for 3 weeks this semester as a part of my class at YY college. Thank you for the opportunity. I observed Stephanie interacting with other children both verbally and in play. She moves about the classroom using her walker and at times holding onto nearby furniture. She especially likes to abandon it when she is playing at the sand and water tables, supporting herself with one arm on the edge, while happily filling and dumping with the other.

CHILD 7: "I am observing in John's class and the teacher asked me to write you a note about my observations. John had another biting episode today. I was surprised that children who are almost 3 years old are still biting. Alexandra stopped crying after her arm was cleaned and she was given a Superman band-aid. Her mother was upset and may be calling you. John keeps biting, probably because he doesn't have the words to tell what he wants and gets frustrated when other children take things away from him. We have been trying to get him to use his words but he hasn't caught on yet. He won't stay in the time-out chair, so that doesn't work. I wonder if you have any suggestions of what works at home? How do you get him to sit in a chair? He really likes playing with the trucks as long as he has the big wooden one, and doesn't throw it like he usually does. He loves to paint, but did splash it around quite a bit when he was making his medieval hat. He doesn't have to sit at the little table by himself anymore. He learned not to eat off of other children's plates when we took his plate away every time he did. That shows how smart he is."

What revisions would you suggest?

_____

_____

Child 7: Oh, where to begin! Of course you know by now that 2 year olds and even 3 year olds do bite! It's part of the stage they're in. And their language expressive skills are still developing. And you would not reveal the details of the incident, especially the names of other children, either of the victim or to the victim. An incident report should be filled out. The family of the injured child receives a copy, but without other children's names written on it. A time-out chair is not an appropriate guidance technique. Throwing a truck indicates that there may not be enough duplicate toys in the classroom, or that there is a lack of supervision. Painting at this age is expected to be messy, but a medieval hat reveals curriculum that is not appropriate for this age. Children cannot be denied food as a punishment nor isolated from other children. The child's behavior does sound typical, but it seems like this program and this student have a lot to learn. Let's try to rewrite it the observation.

I'm a student at YY college and have been observing children in the toddler class at Happy Faces Child Care Center. I've observed John on several occasions and have been working with him closely, assisting him with language and social skills. We have been working on helping him play near other children and adjusting to our self-serve mealtimes. His biggest joys in the class come when he is painting on large pieces of paper and riding on the large wooden trucks.

CHILD 8: "It's been a privilege to observe in Mary Ellen's class to complete my assignments for YY College. The teacher, Ms. Sweetzie, has approved my sharing of my documentation portfolio on Mary Ellen with you. Over the course of the semester, I have observed Mary Ellen's progress, recording it on the school's developmental checklists. I have made focused observations of Mary Ellen in routine classroom activities, and on a portion of the time sample that shows her play choices and attention span (copies attached). Mary Ellen has surpassed the developmental targets in the areas of language and literacy, social and emotional, and small muscle development. She is continuing to develop large muscle coordination skills, an area for which I planned activities for her based on the checklist. She can now walk up and down stairs with alternating feet, is able to skip and gallop for short distances, and has overcome her fear of climbing the ladder on the larger slide on the playground. She (and I) are proud of her accomplishments, as I know you are too. Thanks for a great semester with Mary Ellen and all the best to her in Kindergarten."

What revisions would you suggest?

_____

_____

Child 8: Probably none. It is positive, descriptive, warm in tone, and approved by the teacher.

ISSUES AND TRENDS IN ASSESSMENTS

The field of early childhood education is ever-changing. It is affected by new research on child development and practices to advance development. It is affected by political decisions that attempt to address social issues on federal, state, and local levels. It is impacted by changing demographics of the population, and the widely held value of the sanctity of the family. There is always the tension between the rights and needs of the individual and those of the whole group. Because of these factors, teachers need to participate in professional development throughout their careers to keep informed of issues and trends in the field, and to adapt where necessary. Here are a few issues related to assessment that early childhood teachers face today. Each issue is complex, with research and positions on either side. This overview is just to give you an awareness of the issues, stimulate your own thinking. Further research will solidify your positions on these issues.

NO CHILD LEFT BEHIND

Everyone wants good schools, schools where children can learn what they need to know and be able to succeed in life. In an effort to improve schools, it was necessary to find those that were not producing a standard level of performance. The No Child Left Behind Act of 2002 was a landmark effort to measure school's performance. It was a way to hold schools accountable for how they use federal funding. The schools that are found to have students who perform poorly on standardized tests are given a certain amount of time to improve, or families have the option of moving their children to other schools. Assessment of student achievement using nationally mandated tests became the measuring stick of schools' effectiveness.

Some say that mandatory testing improves students and schools by using an objective measurement, and not one devised by the teacher or the state. Thus, having schools compete to improve is a way to reward the best schools and give parents an idea of which schools are best. The principle is that all children (no matter what their first language, disability, or disadvantage) will be held to the same level of performance on the tests, and this motivates the schools to work harder for these students, and not just push them ahead to the next grade when they have not yet mastered earlier subject matter. When schools and teachers see the high standards that upper grades are expected to know and do, teachers in lower grades will work harder to prepare their students.

The other side of the issue does not disagree that schools need reform to better meet the learning needs of *all* students, but they disagree that nationally mandated testing is the mechanism to achieve that goal. For young children, in the early grades K–3, standardized tests are inappropriate measures of children's learning because of the developmental characteristics of children of this age. No matter what age a child is, standardized tests have been found to contain language and expectations that are often culturally, geographically, and linguistically biased. It is impossible to write tests that are a good fit for such a diverse population. Schools in poverty-stricken areas, without financial resources and plagued by environmental factors such as drugs, gangs, disruptive students, and students whose families do not value education, are further punished. Families in poorly performing schools often do not have the means to transport their children to other schools. The curriculum push-down puts pressure on each lower grade level teacher to "teach to the test" and to teach content that may be of little interest or relevance to the students. Children from diverse backgrounds, languages, poverty, or with learning disabilities are expected to perform at levels beyond their capabilities so they become discouraged, turn into behavior problems, or drop out of school in their teen years.

How will you balance the need for accountability with the advocacy of appropriate assessment methods for measuring outcomes?

MEETING THE NEEDS OF CHILDREN WITH EXCEPTIONALITIES

In the past, children with exceptionalities have been excluded from regular classrooms, placed together no matter what their disabilities, and sometimes overlooked in the belief that everyone deserves an equal education. Laws were enacted that insure that all children have a right to "free and appropriate public education" in the "least restrictive environment," according to an individualized education plan, or IEP (for children under 3, this is called an individualized family service plan, or IFSP), devised by professionals together with the child's family. This inclusion principle recognizes that children are more alike than different, so likenesses should be addressed in a general way for all, while accommodating for differences in a specific way depending on each child's needs.

Children with special needs benefit from an inclusion program in a classroom with developmentally appropriate learning activities and contact with peers who act as role models and become friends. Children without disabilities benefit by early experiences with children who are different from themselves. They can acquire attitudes of acceptance, helping skills, and also benefit from the therapies of special education personnel in the classroom.

A successful inclusion program depends heavily on the teacher's expertise in planning for a diverse group of students. Several studies released in the last few years have noted a gap in the training and education of teachers to support children with special needs in early childhood settings. Other studies have called for a deeper knowledge base in general education as a foundation for all teacher candidates. In schools and early childhood programs, there are increasing challenges to meet the needs of students with disabilities, linguistic differences, or other unique abilities. Also, there are concerns that those children who are included in classrooms will not receive the support and assistance they need. This is the basis for the call for different teacher preparation, one that demands deeper knowledge of general education, child development, pedagogy (how to teach), and special education, as well as expanded in-service professional development and expanded support staff.

More is demanded of teachers, both in preparation and in the workplace, resulting in a high rate of teachers leaving the field in their first 5 years. What will you do to prepare yourself well to plan and include children with differences in your classroom?

AMERICA'S GROWING DIVERSITY

This issue and trend has been mentioned several times in this text, and is emphasized again here. Children in the United States who are enrolled in early childhood programs and in schools look, speak, and act differently than they did 20 or 40 years ago. Those differences will continue to challenge teachers as they strive to meet the needs of the children in their classrooms. Diverse languages, customs, and abilities require teachers to consider every aspect of teaching, from environments to curriculum to celebrations to interactions with families and allied professions. And along with the challenges, of course, comes the expectation of teacher accountability for meeting the learning objectives for each child. Authentic assessment enters into this issue, as well as advocacy, in selecting assessment methods and instruments that are not biased against diverse populations. The teacher must research any mandated instrument for its validity and reliability for the populations served. Fortunately, researchers and test creators are also aware of the diversity challenge and are attempting to take this into consideration. The teacher should be a champion for each and every child.

What are some ways that you can broaden your knowledge of diverse populations and prepare yourself to teach and assess each child in your group fairly?

VIOLENCE IN THE LIVES OF CHILDREN

The statistics of abuse, neglect, and victims of crimes across the United States are staggering. As of 2004, 47 out of 1000 children were investigated for child abuse, with over 11 of those found to be victims. Children younger than age 4 accounted for more than 76 percent of 1400 child abuse fatalities in 2002, according to the Administration for Children and Families report (http://www .childwelfare.gov). Children are victims or witness assaults both in person and through the media at unprecedented rates. Children act out what they see and experience, trying to make sense of it all. As you observe children, you may see them actually recreating or expressing aggression against each other, the teacher, a family member, the environment, and perhaps even you. The younger the child, the greater the threat of violence is to healthy development, both physical and emotional. Your responsibility is to accurately record (write) the details of what you see, and then immediately take either preventative action or give the appropriate assistance. If a child discloses details of abuse, you have an obligation to follow the procedures for reporting the details or the suspicions of abuse or neglect.

On the positive side, you can dedicate yourself to teaching and modeling pro-social and non-violent behavior that includes a commitment to non-punitive methods of child guidance. There are many suggested curricula, including the gentle touch of infants, care of animals, and promoting caring for one another and the environment (for toddlers and older children). The Center on the Social and Emotional Foundations for Early Learning (http://csefel.uiuc.edu) is a resource for technical assistance in this area. Non-punitive child guidance includes an understanding and practice of logical consequences for behavior, non-restraint or denied privileges, and any physical or emotional punishment. Children's media, if used in group settings, should be carefully monitored to eliminate any violent actions, content, or unkindness. Educating families regarding the harmful effects of violence in children's lives is another action that you can take. You can do this by supporting them in positive parenting skills by teaching children non-violent solutions to problems, and protecting them from witnessing media and environmental violence. You can become informed of community efforts and resources to protect children and families from violence.

Think about the ways that you will implement teaching strategies and personal interactions to promote peaceful resolution to problems and to help promote non-violence.

SCHOOL READINESS

The country has repeatedly committed itself to the goal that all children will start school ready to learn. We who know child development know that children are "ready to learn" in the womb and during the early years before formal schooling, when the child is continually learning. This sets the stage for formalized learning in a school setting. This realization of the importance of the early years has resulted in a number of related issues.

Many states are sponsoring pre-kindergarten programs as an investment in children's future learning and as a way of reducing special education costs by identifying and addressing developmental lags earlier. (See www.preknow.org for a comprehensive review.)

■ This identification has led to mandatory screening of children entering kindergarten or pre-kindergarten programs, bringing with it concern over the kinds of tests or screening instruments that are used.

■ There is also concern over the misuse of instruments designed for screening that are used as the sole determinant to deny children kindergarten entrance or to place them in extra-year programs that label them as failures at the outset of their school experience.

■ With the increased emphasis on early literacy and mathematics, there may be curriculum and assessments that are not appropriate for the age/stage of the children.

■ Head Start, a federally funded, comprehensive early childhood program, proposed evaluation for effectiveness based on measurable child outcomes using assessments that may not be developmentally, culturally, or linguistically relevant.

■ The emphasis on school readiness may be causing curriculum "push down," forcing early childhood programs to incorporate academics and assessments that may not be appropriate for the age/stage of the children.

■ Because of the emphasis on early learning, teacher preparation and qualifications are coming under scrutiny for both content and credentialization, focusing on higher education requirements, yet not adjusting salaries to commensurate with the qualifications.

As you can see, there are many school readiness-related issues. There are abundant research studies on each of these issues, although they sometimes contradict one another.

How will you as an early childhood professional use research-based practices to guide your career and classroom decisions?

TECHNOLOGY AND ASSESSMENT

Technology has changed how we communicate, and how we write, store, and retrieve information. With the advent of hand-held computers, it has become possible to manage observation documentation electronically, especially developmental checklists. Individualized curriculum plans based on electronic transfer of developmental checklists are now available. Any written notes are now easily converted to electronic notes through a scanner. Visual depictions of a child's work, paintings, drawings, block structures, dramatic play, and routines all can be captured easily on digital photographs and videos. All of a child's records can be stored electronically, retrieved, sorted, and displayed in a Powerpoint© presentation so easily, that 4 year olds are now doing it.

Communication with families is easier than ever. An e-mail can be sent to individuals, families, or an entire group to quickly convey information, announcements, or greetings. Important messages can be sent and saved through voicemail, eliminating the need for many individual phone calls. Web sites are easily constructed and maintained to present information about the program, children's events, and class progress. Password-protected areas can give families home access to their own child's electronic portfolios and records. Video cameras in classrooms make instant viewing possible for the director, the owner, and individual parents, from home or even from their own offices.

All this available information expands the demands on the teacher for proficiency and time to perform beyond the function of teaching. Communicating with families and the compiling of developmental progress reports are more efficient. The disadvantages are the time it takes to learn about and manipulate documents, and the potential ethical dilemmas concerning the privacy of the child, the classroom, and the program.

It is not the future, it is now! How will you utilize technology to benefit your own learning and the learning and assessment of your students?

REFERENCES

Allen, K. E., & Marotz, L. R. *Developmental profiles: Pre-birth through twelve,* 4th ed. Clifton Park, NY: Thomson Delmar Learning.

Aloha, D., & Kovacik, A. (2006). *Observing and understanding child development: A child study manual.* Clifton Park, NY: Thomson Delmar Learning.

Derman-Sparks, L., & Ramsey, P. (2006). *What if all the kids are white?* New York: Teachers College Press.

Meisels, S. J., & Atkins-Burnett, S. (2005). *Developmental screening in early childhood: A guide,* 5th ed. Washington, DC: National Association for the Education of Young Children.

(2003). *Early childhood curriculum, assessment, and program evaluation position statement with expanded resources.* Washington, DC: National Association for the Education of Young Children (www.naeyc.org).

(2005). *Code of ethical conduct: Statement of commitment.* Washington, DC: National Association for the Education of Young Children (www.naeyc.org).

(2005). *Screening and assessment of young English-language learners.* Washington, DC: National Association for the Education of Young Children (www.naeyc.org).

Nilsen, B. (2007). *Week by week: Documenting young children's development,* 4th ed. Clifton Park, NY: Thomson Delmar Learning.